St. Mich

Cover: *Tapestry displayed on the facade of St. Peter's Basilica, Rome, at the canonization of St. Josemaria Escriva.*

Passionately Loving the World

The Message of St. Josemaria Escriva

edited by

Elmar J. Kremer and Teresa A. Tomory

New York Ottawa Toronto

National Library of Canada Cataloguing in Publication

Passionately loving the world : the message of St. Josemaria Escriva / edited by Elmar J. Kremer and Teresa A. Tomory.

(St. Michael's College series ; 5)
Papers from a conference held at St. Michael's College together with one paper from each of three conferences held in Vancouver, Ottawa and Montreal.
Includes bibliographical references.
ISBN 1-894508-58-0

1. Escrivá de Balaguer, José María, 1902-1975. 2. Escrivá de Balaguer, José Maria, 1902-1975--Congresses. 3. Christian saints--Congresses. I. Kremer, Elmar J. II. Tomory, Teresa A III. Series.

BX4705.E74P37 2004   267'.182'092   C2003-907379-3

For further information and for orders:

http://www.legaspublishing.com

LEGAS
P. O. Box 040328   3 Wood Aster Bay   2908 Dufferin Street
Brooklyn, New York   Ottawa, Ontario   Toronto, Ontario
USA 11204   K2R 1B3   M6B 3S8

Printed and bound in Canada

Contents

PREFACE

Two thousand and two was an eventful year for Opus Dei. January 9 of that year was the one hundredth anniversary of the birth of St. Josemaria Escriva; and many events had been planned to mark the centenary, including a conference to be held at St. Michael's College, University of Toronto, on January 9 and 10, 2003. On December 21, 2001, it was announced that the last step in the process leading up to the canonization of St. Josemaria, a decree of the Holy See recognizing a miracle attributed to his intercession, had been completed; and on February 22, 2002 the date for the canonization was set for October 6, 2002. Thus the conference and other events planned for the centenary became celebrations of the canonization as well.

We publish here the papers of the conference held at St. Michael's College, together with one paper from each of three conferences held in Vancouver, Ottawa, and Montreal. We introduce the volume with a homily of St. Josemaria, "Passionately Loving the World," from which the title of the St. Michael's conference was taken, and conclude with the homily given by Pope John Paul II at the canonization of St. Josemaria in St. Peter's Square, Rome.

We would like to thank those who served with us on the organizing committee for the St. Michael's conference: Ernest Caparros, John Hartley, Paul Kilbertus, Martha Kremer, James T. Roddy, Edward Rzadki, and Paul Tomory. The conference was sponsored by Ernescliff College, a residence for men on the campus of the University of Toronto. The spiritual activities at Ernescliff are entrusted to the Opus Dei Prelature.

PASSIONATELY LOVING THE WORLD[1]

A homily delivered at a Mass celebrated for the Friends
of the University of Navarre on October 8, 1967

You have just been listening to the solemn reading of the two texts of Sacred Scripture for the Mass of the twenty-first Sunday after Pentecost. Having heard the Word of God you are already in the right atmosphere for the words I want to address to you: words of a priest, spoken to a large family of the children of God in his Holy Church. Words, therefore, which are intended to be supernatural, proclaiming the greatness of God and his mercies towards men; words to prepare you for today's great celebration of the Eucharist on the campus of the University of Navarre.

St. Josemaria delivering the homily,
"Passionately Loving the World"

Consider for a moment the event I have just described. We are celebrating the holy Eucharist, the sacramental sacrifice of the Body and Blood of our Lord, that mystery of faith which binds together all the mysteries of Christianity. We are celebrating, therefore, the most sacred and transcendent act which we, men and women, with God's grace can carry out in this life: receiving the Body and Blood of our Lord is, in a certain sense, like loosening our ties with earth and time, so as to be already with God in heaven, where Christ himself will wipe the tears from our eyes and where there will be no more death, nor mourning, nor cries of distress, because the old world will have passed away.[2]

---

[1]Published with the permission of Scepter Publishers, Inc.

[2]See Rev 21:4

This profound and consoling truth, which theologians usually call the eschatological meaning of the Eucharist, could, however, be misunderstood. Indeed, this has happened whenever people have tried to present the Christian way of life as something exclusively *spiritual* — or better, spiritualistic, something reserved for pure, extraordinary people who remain aloof from the contemptible things of this world, or at most tolerate them as something that the spirit just has to live alongside, while we are on this earth.

When people take this approach, churches become the setting *par excellence* of the Christian way of life. And being a Christian means going to church, taking part in sacred ceremonies, getting into an ecclesiastical mentality, in a special kind of world, considered the ante-chamber to heaven, while the ordinary world follows its own separate course. In this case, Christian teaching and the life of grace would pass by, brushing very lightly against the turbulent advance of human history but never coming into proper contact with it.

Encounter Christ in Everyday Life

On this October morning, as we prepare to enter upon the memorial of our Lord's Pasch, we *flatly reject* this deformed vision of Christianity. Reflect for a moment on the setting of our Eucharist, of our Act of Thanksgiving. We find ourselves in a unique temple; we might say that the nave is the University campus; the altarpiece, the University library; over there, the machinery for constructing new buildings; above us, the sky of Navarre...

Surely this confirms in your minds, in a tangible and unforgettable way, the fact that everyday life is the true setting for your lives as Christians. Your daily encounter with Christ takes place where your fellow men, your yearnings, your work and your affections are. It is in the midst of the most material things of the earth that we must sanctify ourselves, serving God and all mankind.

This I have been teaching all the time, using words from holy Scripture: the world is not evil, because it comes from the hands of God, because it is his creation, because Yahweh looked upon it and saw that it was good.[3] It is we ourselves, men and women, who make it evil and ugly with our sins and unfaithfulness. Don't doubt it, my children: any attempt to escape from the noble reality of daily life is, for you men and women of the world, something opposed to the will of God.

God in the Ordinary

On the contrary, you must realise now, more clearly than ever, that God is calling you to serve him in and from the ordinary, secular and civil activities of human life. He waits for us everyday, in the laboratory, in the operating theatre, in the army barracks, in the university chair, in the factory, in the workshop, in the fields, in the home and in all the immense panorama of work. Understand this well: there is *something* holy, something divine hidden in the most ordinary situations, and it is up to each one of you to discover it.

---

[3]See Gen 1:7 ff.

I often said to the university students and workers who were with me in the 'thirties that they had to know how to *materialize* their spiritual lives. I wanted to warn them of the temptation, so common then and now, to lead a kind of double life: on the one hand, an inner life, a life related to God; and on the other, as something separate and distinct, their professional, social and family lives, made up of small earthly realities.

No, my children! We cannot lead a double life. We cannot be like schizophrenics, if we want to be Christians. There is only one life, made of flesh and spirit. And it is that life which has to become, in both body and soul, holy and filled with God: we discover the invisible God in the most visible and material things.

There is no other way, my daughters and sons: either we learn to find our Lord in ordinary, everyday life, or we shall never find him. That is why I tell you that our age needs to give back to matter and to the apparently trivial events of life their noble, original meaning. It needs to place them at the service of the Kingdom of God; it needs to spiritualize them, turning them into a means and an occasion for a continuous meeting with Jesus Christ.

Christian Materialism

The genuine Christian approach —which professes the resurrection of all flesh— has always quite logically opposed 'dis-incarnation' without fear of being judged materialistic. We can, therefore, rightly speak of a *Christian materialism*, which is boldly opposed to those materialisms which are blind to the spirit.

What are the sacraments, which people in early times described as the footprints of the Incarnate Word, if not the clearest expression of this way which God has chosen in order to sanctify us and to lead us to heaven? Don't you see that each sacrament is the love of God, with all its creative and redemptive power, given to us through the medium of material things? What is this Eucharist which we are about to celebrate if not the Adorable Body and Blood of our Redeemer, which is offered to us through the lowly matter of this world (wine and bread), through the elements of nature, cultivated by man[4] as the recent Ecumenical Council has reminded us.

It is understandable, my children, that the Apostle should write: "All things are yours, you are Christ's and Christ is God's."[5] We have here an ascending movement which the Holy Spirit, poured into our hearts, wants to call forth in this world: upwards from the earth to the glory of the Lord. And to make it clear that in such a movement everything is included, even what seems most commonplace, St Paul also wrote: "In eating, in drinking, do everything for God's glory."[6]

---

[4]See Vatican Council II, Pastoral Constitution, *Gaudium et spes,* no. 38.

[5]1 Cor 3:22-23.

[6]1 Cor 10:31.

This doctrine of Sacred Scripture, as you know, is to be found in the very core of the spirit of Opus Dei. It should lead you to do your work perfectly, to love God and your fellowmen by putting love in the little things of everyday life, and discovering that *divine something* which is hidden in small details. The lines of a Castillian poet are especially appropriate here: "Write slowly and with a careful hand, for doing things well is more important than doing them."[7]

Heroic Verse Out of Prose

I assure you, my children, that when a Christian carries out with love the most insignificant everyday action, that action overflows with the transcendence of God. That is why I have told you so often, and hammered away at it, that the Christian vocation consists in making heroic verse out of the prose of each day. Heaven and earth seem to merge, my children, on the horizon. But where they really meet is in your hearts, when you sanctify your everyday lives...

I have just said, sanctify your everyday lives. And with these words I refer to the whole programme of your task as Christians. Stop dreaming. Leave behind false idealisms, fantasies, and what I usually call *mystical wishful thinking*: If only I hadn't married; if only I had a different job or qualification; if only I were in better health; if only I were younger; if only I were older.[8] Instead, turn to the most material and immediate reality, which is where our Lord is: "Look at my hands and my feet, said the risen Jesus, be assured that it is myself; touch me and see; a spirit has not flesh and bones, as you see that I have.[9]

Lay Outlook

Light is shed upon many aspects of the world in which you live, when you start from these truths. Take your activity as citizens, for instance. A man who knows that the world —and not just the church— is the place where he finds Christ, loves that world. He endeavours to become properly trained, intellectually and professionally. He makes up his own mind, in full freedom, about the problems of the environment in which he moves, and he takes his own decisions in consequence. As the decisions of a Christian, they derive from personal reflection, which strives in all humility to grasp the will of God in both the unimportant and the important events of his life.

But it never occurs to such a Christian to think or say that he was stepping down from the temple into the world to represent the Church, or that his solu-

---

[7]A. Machado, *Poesias Completas*, vol. 159; *Proverios y cantares,* 24.(Madrid: Espasa Calpe, 1940):
Despacito, y buena letra:
el hacer las cosas bien
importa más que le hacerlas.

[8]Translator's Note: A play on words between *ojala* ("would that", "if only") and *hojalata* ("tin-plate"). *Mística ojalatera* is "tin-can mysticism" as well as 'mystical wishful thinking."

[9]Luke 24:39.

tions are *the Catholic solutions* to the problems. That would be completely inadmissible! That would be clericalism, *official Catholicism*, or whatever you want to call it. In any case, it means doing violence to the very nature of things. What you must do is foster a real *lay mentality*, which will lead to three conclusions:

— be honourable enough to shoulder your own personal responsibility;
— be Christian enough to respect those brothers in the faith who, in matters of free discussion, propose solutions which differ from yours; and,
— be Catholic enough not to make a tool of our Mother the Church, involving her in human factions.

Responsible Freedom

It is obvious that, in this field as in all others, you would not be able to carry out this programme of sanctifying your everyday life if you did not enjoy all the freedom which proceeds from your dignity as men and women created in the image of God, and which the Church freely recognizes. Personal freedom is essential for the Christian life. But do not forget, my sons, that I always speak of a responsible freedom.

Interpret, then, my words as what they are: a call to exercise your rights every day, and not just in times of emergency. A call to fulfil honourably your commitments as citizens in all fields — in politics and in financial affairs, in university life and in your job — accepting with courage all the consequences of your free decisions and shouldering the personal independence which is yours. A Christian *lay outlook* of this sort will enable you to flee from all intolerance, from all fanaticism. To put it positively, it will help you live in peace with all your fellow citizens, and to promote understanding and harmony in the various spheres of social life.

I know I have no need to remind you of something which I have been saying for so many years. This doctrine of civic freedom, of understanding, of living in harmony with other people, forms a very important part of the message spread by Opus Dei. Must I affirm once again that the men and women who want to serve Jesus Christ in the Work of God, are simply citizens *the same as everyone else*, who strive to live their Christian vocation to its ultimate consequences with a deep sense of responsibility?

Nothing distinguishes my children from their fellow citizens. On the other hand, apart from the faith they share, they have nothing in common with the members of religious congregations. I love the religious, and I venerate and admire their apostolates, their cloister, their separation from the world, their *contemptus mundi*, which are *other* signs of holiness in the Church. But the Lord has not given me a religious vocation, and for me to desire it would not be in order. No authority on earth can force me to be a religious, just as no authority can make me marry. I am a secular priest: a priest of Jesus Christ who is passionately in love with the world.

Solidarity Through Work

These are the men and women who have followed Jesus Christ in the company of this poor sinner: a small percentage of priests, who have previously exercised a secular profession or trade; a large number of secular priests from many dioceses throughout the world, who in this way confirm their obedience to their respective bishops, their love for their diocesan work and the effectiveness of it. Their arms are always wide open, in the form of a cross, to make room in their hearts for all souls; and like myself they live in the hustle and bustle of the workaday world which they love. And finally, a great multitude made up of men and women of different nations, and tongues, and races, who earn their living with their work. Most of them are married, many others single; they share with their fellow citizens in the important task of making temporal society more human and more just. And they work as I have said, shoulder to shoulder with their fellow men, experiencing with them successes and failures in the noble struggle of daily endeavour, as they strive to fulfil their duties and to exercise their social and civic rights. And all this with naturalness, like any other conscientious Christian, without considering themselves special. Blended into the mass of their companions, they try at the same time to detect the flashes of divine splendour which shine through the commonest everyday realities.

Similarly the activities which are promoted by Opus Dei as an association have these eminently secular characteristics: they are not ecclesiastical activities — they do not in any way represent the hierarchy of the Church. They are the fruit of human, cultural and social initiatives of ordinary citizens who try to make them reflect the light of the Gospel and to bring them the warmth of Christ's love. An example which will help to make this clear is that Opus Dei does not, and never will, undertake the task of directing diocesan seminaries, in which bishops *instituted by the Holy Spirit*[10] train their future priests.

Eminently Secular

Opus Dei on the other hand, does foster technical training centres for industrial workers, agricultural training schools for farm labourers, centres for primary, secondary and university education, and many other varied activities all over the world, because its apostolic zeal, as I wrote many years ago, is like a sea without shores.

But what need have I to speak at length on this topic, when your very presence here is more eloquent than a long address? You, Friends of the University of Navarre, are part of a body of people who know it is committed to the progress of the broader society to which it belongs. Your sincere encouragement, your prayers, sacrifices and contributions are not offered on the basis of Catholic confessionalism. Your cooperation is a clear testimony of a well-formed social conscience, which is concerned with the temporal common good. You are witnesses to the fact that a university can be born of the energies of the people and be sustained by the people.

[10]Acts 20:28

On this occasion, I want to offer my thanks once again for the cooperation lent to our University, by my noble city of Pamplona, by the region of Navarre, by the Friends of the University from every part of Spain and — I say this with particular feeling — by people who are not Spaniards, even by people who are not Catholics or Christians, who have understood the purpose and spirit of this enterprise and have shown it with their active help.

Thanks to all of them this University has grown ever more effective as a focus of civic freedom, of intellectual training, of professional endeavour, and a stimulus for university education generally. Your generous sacrifice is part of the foundation of this whole undertaking which seeks to promote the human sciences, social welfare and the teaching of the faith.

What I have just pointed out has been clearly understood by the people of Navarre, who also recognise that their University is a factor in the economic development and, especially, in the social advancement of the region; a factor which has given so many of their children an opportunity to enter the intellectual professions which, otherwise, would have been difficult and, in some cases, impossible to obtain. This awareness of the role which the University would play in their lives is surely what inspired the support which Navarre has lent it from the beginning — support which will undoubtedly keep on growing in enthusiasm and extent.

I continue to harbour the hope —because it accords both with the requirements of justice and with the practice which obtains in so many countries— that the time will come when the Spanish government will contribute its share to lighten the burden of an undertaking which seeks no private profit, but on the contrary is totally dedicated to the service of society, and tries to work efficiently for the present and future prosperity of the nation.

Noble Human Love

And now, my sons and daughters, let me consider another aspect of everyday life which is particularly dear to me. I refer to human love, to the noble love between a man and a woman, to courtship and marriage. I want to say once again that this holy human love is not something to be merely permitted or tolerated alongside the true activities of the spirit, as might be insinuated by those false spiritualisms which I referred to earlier. I have been preaching and writing just the very opposite for forty years, and now those who did not understand are beginning to grasp the point.

Love, which leads to marriage and family, can also be a marvellous divine way, a vocation, a path for a complete dedication to our God. Do things perfectly, I have reminded you. Put love into the little duties of each day; discover that *divine something* contained in these details. All this teaching has a special place in that area of life where human love has its setting.

All of you who are lecturers or students or who work in any capacity in the University of Navarre know that I have entrusted your love to Mary, Mother of Fair Love. And here, on the university campus, you have the shrine which we

St. JosemariaEscriva at the University of Navarre, October 9, 1967.

built so devoutly, as a place to receive your prayers and the offering of that wonderful and pure love on which she bestows her blessing."Surely you know that your bodies are the shrines of the Holy Spirit, who is God's gift to you, so that you are no longer your own masters?"[11] How often, before the statue of the Blessed Virgin, of the Mother of Fair Love, will you not reply to the Apostle's question with a joyful affirmation: Yes, we know that this is so and we want to live it with your powerful help, O Virgin Mother of God.

Contemplative prayer will rise within you whenever you meditate on this impressive truth: something as material as my body has been chosen by the Holy Sprit as his dwelling place... I no longer belong to myself... My body and soul, my whole being, belong to God... And this prayer will be rich in practical results arising from the great consequence which the Apostle himself suggests: *glorify God in your bodies.*[12]

Besides, you cannot fail to realise that only among those who understand and value in all its depth what we have just considered about human love, can there arise another ineffable insight of which Jesus speaks:[13] an insight which is a pure gift of God, moving a person to surrender body and soul to the Lord, to offer him an undivided heart, without the mediation of earthly love.

Holiness in Everyday Life

I must finish now, my children. I said at the beginning that I wanted to tell you something of the greatness and mercy of God. I think I have done so in speaking to you about sanctifying your everyday life. A holy life in the midst of secular affairs, lived without fuss, with simplicity, with truthfulness: is this not today the most moving manifestation of the *magnalia Dei*,[14] of those prodi-

---

[11] 1 Cor 6:19.
[12] 1 Cor 6:20.
[13] Mt 19:11.
[14] Sir 18:4.

gious mercies which God has always worked and still works, in order to save the world?

Now, with the Psalmist I ask you to join in my prayer and in my praise: *Magnificate Dominum mecum, et extollamus nomen eius simul*[15] — praise the Lord with me, let us extol his name together. In other words, my children, let us live by faith.

Let us take up the shield of faith, the helmet of salvation and the sword of the Spirit, which is God's Word. That is what St Paul encourages us to do in the epistle to the Ephesians,[16] which was read in the liturgy a few moments ago.

Faith is a virtue which we Christians greatly need, and in a special way in this 'Year of Faith' which our beloved Holy Father Pope Paul VI has decreed. For, without faith, we lack the very foundation for the sanctification of ordinary life.

A living faith in these moments, because we are drawing near to the *mysterium fidei*,[17] to the Holy Eucharist: because we are about to participate in our Lord's Pasch, which sums up and effects the mercies of God towards men.

Faith, my children, in order to acknowledge that within a few *moments the work of our Redemption*[18] is going to be renewed on this altar. Faith, to savour the Creed and to experience, around this altar and in this Assembly, the presence of Christ, who makes us *cor unum et anima una*,[19] one heart and one soul and transforms us into a family, a Church which is one, holy, catholic, apostolic and Roman, which for us is the same as saying universal.

Faith, finally, my beloved daughters and sons, to show the world that all this is not just ceremonies and words, but a divine reality, as we present to mankind the testimony of an ordinary life made holy, in the name of the Father and of the Son and of the Holy Spirit and of Holy Mary.

---

[15] Ps 33:4.

[16] Eph 6:11 ff.

[17] 1 Tim 3:9.

[18] Prayer over the Offerings, Mass of the Ninth Sunday after Pentecost.

[19] Acts 4:32.

JOHN M. HAAS

PASSIONATELY LOVING THE WORLD, THE MESSAGE OF ST. JOSEMARIA

To love the world passionately. This is what God has called us to do through the example and teaching of his saint, Josemaria Escriva. To love the world passionately.

However, this is a "hard saying" for many Catholics in our day. We are to love the world. Yet we live in a broken world with millions of abortions committed every year, with our societies awash in pornography, with even

John Haas at St. Michael's College,
University of Toronto, January 10, 2003.

Catholic couples undergoing surgical sterilizations, with record numbers of out-of-wedlock pregnancies and venereal diseases, with fierce media assaults upon the Church and her teachings, with human embryos being engendered for destructive research, with attempts at human cloning. How do we passionately love this world? After all, should we not repudiate "the world, the flesh and the devil"?

St. Josemaria, who called us to love the world passionately, was himself no stranger to the disorder and ugliness of fallen humanity. He lived in a world with totalitarian regimes repressing and murdering the innocent by the millions; he lived in a world suffering the unspeakable cruelties of the Spanish Civil War; he knew priests and women religious who were brutally murdered by Communists. As a youth he prayed a lot for Christians persecuted in Mexico and for Catholics in Ireland.

The founder of Opus Dei witnessed the dangers of the Civil War first-hand and indeed suffered from them himself. St. Josemaria had to go about in disguises, travel at night, use code language. On one occasion it was thought he had been killed when friends saw a body resembling his hanging from a tree just outside his home.

On another occasion in 1936 he was in hiding in an apartment. The militia began searching the houses on the street, beginning in the cellars and going to the attics floor by floor. St. Josemaria and others fled to the attic of their building. Of course he was not wearing clerical garb, and one of his party did not even know he was a priest. As they huddled in the hot, dusty attic, they could hear the militia in the attic next door. In this very dangerous situation, Father Josemaria approached one of the men hiding with him and said, "I am a priest. We are in difficult times. If you want, you can make an act of contrition, and I will give you absolution."

Revealing himself as a priest could have meant death for St. Josemaria. Indeed, the man to whom he had offered absolution could have betrayed him to try to save his own life. Fortunately it did not come to that. The point is that St. Josemaria knew well, he had ample experience of, the evils of a fallen world.

Before, during and after the war, he suffered false accusations and calumnies from his own brothers in the Faith, which was particularly painful for him. And as we do today, he lived in a world of increasing divorce, spreading public immorality, desertions from the priesthood in the thousands. As we know, he condemned the fruits of this *fallen* world in language as harsh as any used by Old Testament prophets or by Our Lord Himself, who excoriated the religious leaders of his day as white washed sepulchers and broods of vipers. Yet, remarkably, it was still this world he called on us to love passionately.

How is this apparent contradiction to be resolved? What exactly *is* the world St. Josemaria calls us to love so passionately? The answer to that question might help us understand the message of this newly canonized saint and in turn help us in our struggle to build the civilization of love to which our Holy Father has called us.

As noted, St. Josemaria was no stranger to a world suffering from the harsh effects of sin. But he was even more intimate with the world as God created it, as God intended it to be, and as He redeemed it in Christ. St. Josemaria loved this world because he knew and understood it from a supernatural perspective; he saw it in its relation to its Creator and its Redeemer.

In his 1967 homily at the University of Navarre, entitled "Passionately Loving the World", St. Josemaria reminded us of a profound Catholic truth, a truth of which we cannot be reminded too often: What God created is good. And this good world coming from the hand of God was created for the crown of creation, for man. When the world was sullied through human sin, it was restored in Christ and elevated to previously unimaginable heights — again, for the sake of man.

It is precisely this world, for which Christ poured out His life's blood, that St. Josemaria loved so much as a son of the God who brought this world into being out of nothing for the sake of love. The Founder of Opus Dei deeply understood the words of the Evangelist John: "For God so loved the world that he gave His only begotten Son that everyone who believes in Him should not die, but have eternal life" (John 3:16).

This was the world St. Josemaria knew and loved — through the grime and the filth of human sin. The theologians tell us that we are to love the sinner, not "as sinner" but rather as a potential friend of God. We are never to love Satan and the fallen angels because they can never become friends of God, but the sinner can. It is human nature only to love that which is good and which has the potential to be good. St. Josemaria had a supernatural vision which allowed him to see the good wherever it was and to love every sinner he encountered —who was everyone he encountered (!)— as a potential friend of God.

The story is told of the father of a prostitute in Madrid who was dying in the brothel where the daughter lived. Friends came to Father Escriva asking him to administer the last rites to the dying man. The saint could have refused to enter such a vile establishment but he knew there was a soul in need of redemption, who, like the thief upon the cross, could be snatched from Satan and stolen away to heaven, even at the last moment. St. Josemaria said he would come, but only on the condition that the sinful activity which occurred in that place cease the day before and the day after.

It is interesting to note that St. Josemaria did not place such a heavy demand that it may not have been met, and the dying man deprived of his last chance of salvation. But on the other hand, he did not act as though he were indifferent to the sinful activity taking place in that house. He insisted that it cease for a while almost as though a truce had been called between the warring factions of good and evil, so that the priest could make his way to the battlefield to anoint a poor soul wounded and dying. What always struck me about that story is that St. Josemaria saw a potential friend of God in that dying man and did his utmost to reach him before it was too late.

But the virtues of prudence and fortitude which the founder of Opus Dei manifested on that occasion were won with struggle and hard work. Virtues work as second natures in us, but they do not come naturally. They must be formed. If we would be entirely honest about this holy man, we would have to acknowledge that it was not easy for St. Josemaria to control his anger and to be meek. But his anger was not a disorder; it was the virtue of righteous indignation. He became angry with injustice, sinfulness, disorder. When one reads through his aphorisms and counsels in *The Way*, *The Forge* or *The Furrow*, one is often struck by his brutal frankness. He will reassure his spiritual charges with soothing words, such as "Forgive my sincerity ..."[1] or "Don't be angry if I tell you ...",[2] and then he will go on to hit them with characterizations of their attitudes or behaviors which are remarkably severe.

We read, for example, in the *Furrow*, 708: "Malicious, suspicious, devious, mistrustful, grudging . . . these are all adjectives which you deserve, even though they might annoy you." "Might annoy you!?" I dare say, if my spiritual director ever said such things to me, I would be devastated. But St. Josemaria did not mince words in his fraternal corrections. He did not mince words because he loved his spiritual children, and he knew full well just how serious

---

[1] *Furrow*, 600.

[2] *Furrow*, 706

is the spiritual struggle in which we are all engaged. The stakes could not be higher. They are, frankly, eternal bliss and happiness or eternal damnation and torment.

The Founder of the Work wanted us to love that which is truly good, not some counterfeit good; he wanted us to love the world God created and Christ re-created. This is the world which we are to love passionately and which we are to help bring to its promised fullness in Christ. And in the estimation of St. Josemaria, nothing we know lies outside this lovable world, either as already worthy of love or as having the potential to be worthy of our love.

St. Josemaria respected and admired the vocation to religious life; he particularly venerated contemplatives. But he knew that most of us called to be followers of Christ have the vocation to live in the world, not apart from it. This world is not to be feared but to be loved and through that love this world is to be transformed according to the mind of Christ. Clearly we are not to love the disorder which human greed and pride and sensuality have managed to engender but we *are* to love that which God intends the world to be. And this gives us another profound insight into the thought of St. Josemaria, since it takes a contemplative soul to be able to see reality for what it truly is, as it has proceeded from the hand of God—and what it can be as we unite it to our prayer and our acts of love for God. We hear St. Josemaria saying over and over: "I will never tire of repeating that we have to be contemplative souls in the midst of the world, who try to convert their work into prayer."[3]

It is instructive that St. Josemaria does not simply speak of praying while one works but rather of actually converting work into prayer. Our work, our daily professional or domestic work, becomes the means of our sanctification, of our growing in holiness, of our becoming more fully one with God in Jesus Christ. St. Josemaria liked to reflect on the hidden life of Christ as being particularly edifying for us.

Jesus was engaged in His redemptive work even before His public ministry began. At that time he was perceived as the ordinary son of Mary and Joseph, working in the carpentry shop, attending the synagogue, celebrating at wedding feasts with his friends, fulfilling his religious obligations by going up to Jerusalem. All of these ordinary activities were so ordinary in fact, that none of the evangelists take note of them. They were indeed so ordinary that the neighbors were perplexed by Him when He began His public ministry. Yet despite their ordinariness, His daily chores and activities were ineffably extraordinary acts bringing about the redemption of the world. They were redemptive acts precisely because they were joined to the Person and the Mission of the Incarnate Son of God—just as our ordinary deeds can be redemptive of the world as we offer them to the Father in union with His Son.

The motto of Benedictine monks is "Ora et Labora (Prayer and Work)". As a motto for Opus Dei, we might suggest "Ora per Laborem (Work as Prayer)". Our life is not bifurcated into mundane work and spiritual work. Rather, St.

---

3 *Furrow*, 497

Josemaria meant it quite literally when he said, "Pray without ceasing." Our work and activities can be a prayer if they are offered up to God and done with a supernatural motive.

I must say, I think this truth of the thought of St. Josemaria is difficult to grasp precisely because of its simplicity. When Naaman, the Syrian general, turned to the Prophet Elisha seeking to be cleansed from his leprosy, he was prepared to do extraordinary things. Yet all the prophet told him to do was to go bathe in the Jordan. Naaman was furious. He was prepared to do so much more. He was a courageous and important man! Was the prophet mocking him?

The message of Josemaria may at times seem even a little disappointing, as Elisha's did to Naaman. "Is that all I am to do to be raised to the altar? To be a saint? Simply my daily chores, my daily work? Helping my wife with the dishes? Repairing the garage door? Making sure the data I am using in my research is correct and not tainted? Helping my son with homework? Attending the parent-teacher conference for our daughter? Please, Lord. I am ready to do so much more. I am ready to embrace martyrdom, to witness to you before the mighty of the world." And then St. Josemaria whispers to us Our Lord's own words. "Because you have been "in pauca fidelis' – 'faithful in the little things' – enter into the joy of your Lord. The words are Christ's. 'In pauca fidelis!...' Now will you disdain little things, if heaven itself is promised to those who keep them?"[4] The little things. Indeed, guarding our tongue from a malicious, but delicious, piece of gossip can be a martyrdom of sorts. Not succumbing to a particularly seductive sensual temptation may actually be more difficult, and require more fortitude, than witnessing to the faith before a persecuting Caesar.

I had known the Work for several years before I began to grasp the real significance of the teaching of St. Josemaria in this area. I had had a consulting contract with the Department of Justice in the Reagan Administration. At the time I was offered the position of chief financial officer of a Catholic college and seminary. I was struggling with what I should do, stay with my current position or pursue the new one. Over lunch one day with a member of the Work, a numerary, I mentioned that I thought I would probably take the position with the Catholic college and seminary, since I had always wanted to serve the Church. I was startled when he suddenly slammed his fist on the table repeatedly and shouted, "No! No! No! You don't get it! You just don't get it. You ARE the Church. You serve the Church most effectively by advancing your own professional work, by doing your professional work well. *That* is serving our Lord and His Church."

This is a difficult lesson to learn, since we invariably fall into the trap of thinking that we truly serve the Church only in some institutional or quasi-clerical role. It is thought that the earnest Catholic is the one who enters the sanctuary to be a lector or an extraordinary minister of the Holy Eucharist or who enters into some position with the institutional church. But St. Josemaria and

[4]*The Way*, 819; cf. Mt. 25:21.

his children know that is not the case. Whether we are preparing a legal brief, doing stock analysis, or selling an automobile, our work itself can become a prayer and a means of sanctification. The truth is profound in its simplicity. As Our Father said in *The Way*, 359: "Add a supernatural motive to your ordinary professional work, and you will have sanctified it." No need for a religious habit, no need for a monastery or retreat house, no need, even, for a weekend away. At 10:30 on a Monday morning at your desk on Wabash Street in Chicago, or Park Avenue South in New York or Walnut Street in Philadelphia or Bay Street in Toronto, you can and should be engaged in sanctifying yourself and the world through your daily work.

However, we must remember that doing our work with care, with attention, with professionalism will not accomplish our desired purposes if we are not in a state of grace, if we are not in close friendship with God. St. Josemaria uses a wonderful image to make this point. He says that without grace we are no more effective in our work than a busy, industrious seamstress who feverishly sews all day but with no thread in her needle. However, if the needle is threaded, if we are in a state of grace, what magnificent garments we can engender.

With God's grace, with attention to the details of ordinary life, with a supernatural motive of love in all we do, with an awareness of our own dignity and the dignity of all whom we meet because of our being children of the same Father God, we can wrest from the hand of Satan one piece of fallen territory after another.

I believe that a considerable portion of the genius of St. Josemaria and of Opus Dei is the embrace of the virtue of patience. We see it in abundance when Our Father writes of tribulations, of the interior struggle and of hope.

St. Josemaria knew that nothing can be accomplished without integrity and without God's grace. He knew that, fundamentally, they were all that really mattered. The Work is not and cannot be a "mass movement". It provides personal, individualized formation to help one soul grow in holiness, and another and another. And those souls will help still others grow in holiness, their spouses, their children, their colleagues, their employees, their students. It is an historical fact that the loss of Christendom and the subsequent social disorder were long in coming. The civilization of love and life for which we now struggle and for which we yearn will likewise be long in coming. But it will come only as your life and my life and each particular life are lived in conformity with the mind of Christ.

Moses was never able to enter the Promised Land. St. Josemaria never lived to see the establishment of the personal prelature toward which he groped and worked his entire adult life. John Paul II will not live to see the emergence of the civilization of love and life for which he has struggled so indefatigably. I will never see it either. But there is a sense in which that does not matter. It is not ours to engender but God's. And the sanctified activities which we undertake even now have themselves an eternal significance and build toward that new Christian civilization which will flourish in God's time. But it will be done in God's time, not ours, which is why the virtue of patience is so important.

"Black Robe" is a moving film made about the work of the French Jesuit missionaries among the Native Americans here in Canada. It is a rough movie, entirely unromantic in its presentation of the deprivations, the sufferings, the tortures, the agonies, and the eventual death endured by many of these Jesuits. Finally, after the most arduous efforts and the most heroic of sacrifices, an Indian village is converted and all the villagers are baptized. Yet at the conclusion of the movie, a post-script written across the screen informs the audience that the entire village was annihilated the following year by a hostile neighboring tribe. Without a supernatural vision, all that effort could be seen as futile, indeed, as unspeakably useless, ineffectual, an unbelievable wastage of human life and talent. But with a supernatural vision, that effort must be understood as supremely effective, as ultimately successful.

Our Father wrote in *The Way*, 691: "Are you suffering some great tribulation? . . . Say very slowly, as if savoring the words, this powerful and manly prayer: 'May the most just and most lovable will of God be done, be fulfilled, be praised and eternally exalted above all things. Amen. Amen.' I assure you that you'll find peace." And that is all that matters. That the most just most lovable will of God be done. That is it. That was the mission that Christ came to accomplish; simply, the Will of His Father. That is the mission for every Christian, to be a co-redeemer, to be an "*alter Christus*"

We carry out our baptismal vows working to transform society according to the mind of Christ. Virgil had declared: "*Tantae molis erat Romanam condere gentem*"—"Such a toil it was to found the Roman people." It will be an even greater toil to found in our day a Christian civilization of love and life. But this is what we have been called to work for, unsparingly.

We struggle and work and pray for the establishment of a civilization of love and life, but not as some abstraction. We do not have a love for humanity in general. (Indeed, save me from the man who does.) Rather we love our spouses and our children. We love our neighbors, our friends, our countrymen. They have names and they have faces. Each is a unique child of God eliciting from us an act of love and an acknowledgment of his or her dignity.

Many years ago I was visiting a dear friend who was serving as the United States Ambassador to Guatemala. It was a time of terrible bloodshed in Guatemala, still known as "La Violencia". My friend offered to provide me with an embassy car and driver, but in light of the fact that one of his predecessors had been assassinated, I respectfully declined. I did not want to be a slow-moving and conspicuous American target in a land torn by violence. I said I would be perfectly happy to take a taxi!

I was directed to the closest taxi stand. However, when I arrived at the location, there was not a taxi to be seen. There were only a number of beat-up old cars parked on the grass under the shade of a large tree. I walked to the edge of what appeared to be a graveyard for abandoned cars. I raised my voice and shouted out hesitatingly: "Taxi". Suddenly half a dozen men leapt to their feet from the shade of the trees, or rolled out of their cars. I had found the taxi stand.

I chose an old, rusty, dented Chevrolet with a driver who looked little better. He was missing teeth, was unshaven, was wearing wrinkled clothes and sandals without socks. When I found out how little he charged, I engaged him as my driver for the entire stay.

The gear shift had long ago broken off the steering column, but he had made a primitive one which he had attached to the gear box through a hole he had cut in the floor. Whenever he had to go in reverse, white smoke billowed out of the tail pipe enveloping the car. I have no idea how he managed to see where we were going in reverse.

I always rode in the front seat with him, and we talked about many things. Politics, international affairs, the weekly radio shows of the current dictator, Rios Mont, the importance of family. He had a strong sense of justice and of private property. One day he pointed at my brief case. "Nice brief case," he said. "You bought that with your own money." "Yes, I did," I said. "You worked hard for that money," he said. "Yes, I did," I responded. "That nice brief case belongs to you and you are entitled to it." "That's right," I said. He nodded in agreement. Another day, we had a similar conversation about my suit.

Eventually our discussions turned to religion. Evangelical sects were making strong inroads into Guatemala. In fact, the dictator at the time was Evangelical. "You Christian?" he asked me. "Yes, I am," I answered. "As a matter of fact, I'm Catholic." "What kind?" he asked. This was a time of the influence of liberation theology in Latin America. It was a movement which was heavily influenced by Marxist thought and which tried to set up a parallel People's Catholic Church to the Roman Catholic Church. I turned the question around on him. "What kind of Catholic are *you*?" I asked. "Me? I'm a true Catholic," he said, and to impress upon me just how true a Catholic he was he lowered the visor above the windshield and pulled out a prayer card to the Venerable Josemaria Escriva. "Un catolico verdadero! A true Catholic," he declared. Not to be outdone, I took my wallet out of my suitcoat pocket and pulled out my prayer card to Josemaria. "Hey, hermano (brother)," he exclaimed. "Hey, mano a mano", roughly translated, "Hey, brother, shake!" The conversation became very warm and very animated. He wanted to know how many children my wife and I had, their ages, their names, and he told me all about their children.

When I finally left Guatemala, we promised one another our prayers. As we stood on the sidewalk beside his beat-up old Chevrolet and took our leave of one another, he told me to give each of our girls a kiss from him and each of our boys "un abrazo", an embrace. His love was concrete, it was personalized. It was the love that would build a Christian civilization.

My Guatemalan friend had called me "brother" because we were children of the same Father God. It is the reality of divine filiation, of our being God's children, that bestows dignity on us. The teaching of St. Josemaria on divine filiation is usually seen in light of its implications for personal piety and for the interior struggle of individuals as they grow in holiness. However, the teaching also has profound implications for communal life, for social policy, and for the shaping of a culture of life. St. Josemaria was always aware that it was individuals living and working and worshiping and growing toward holiness who *together* would give rise to a just and humane society.

It is a Christian reality that as individuals grow in holiness, as they become aware of their own vocation to sanctity, as they faithfully fulfill their own professional and personal lives, they contribute more effectively toward a humane culture with public policies respectful of the dignity of the weak and vulnerable in their midst.

The greater the awareness of the loving goodness of God and of the divine source of all human life, the more just and humane will be the institutions of any society. This insight is not limited to Catholics, since every human person has been created in God's image and likeness. Even those who do not share our Catholic faith should be able to be aware of the unique quality of human life. The human characteristic which ought to prove to our contemporaries who do not share our faith that the human person has a transcendent, divine origin is the human capacity to love, to form friendships, to care for and to sacrifice for others. And we are the ones who can provide that proof to them.

In his emphasis on divine filiation, St. Josemaria taught a truth which even non-Christians should be able to intuit. Human life does not define itself. It does not provide the ground of its own being or a rationale for its own value. Human life enjoys a participatory value. Human life is a reflection of that which is goodness itself, truth itself, life itself. As Blessed Josemaria wrote: "(A son of God). . . says to himself: God is my Father and he is the Author of all good; he is all Goodness."[5] Pope John Paul II expresses the same truth when he teaches: "Man has been given a sublime dignity, based on the intimate bond which unites him to his Creator: in man there shines forth a reflection of God himself."[6]

Regrettably, in our day a human being becomes valuable only when he is deemed to be valuable by those who have ultimate control over his life or death. Parents decide whether a so-called defective child is worth bringing to term. Indeed, in some societies, parents decide whether a girl baby or a boy baby is worth bringing to birth.

Scientists in laboratories decide which embryo in a petri dish is worth implanting and which ones will be discarded or subjected to experimentation. If we approach human life as crass materialists who deny any transcendent, spiritual dimension to human life, then no criteria other than materialist ones can be applied to moral decisions with respect to such life. If there is no intrin-

---

[5] *The Forge*, 987.

[6] John Paul II, *The Gospel of Life*, 34.

sic value to human life derived from its reflecting the divine image destined for fellowship with God, then the way in which we relate to human life will be determined by criteria external to human life itself. The criterion by which a human being lives or dies becomes virtually and inevitably utilitarian.

The decision of those who have the power is calculated on what, in their estimation, will bring about the greatest good for the greatest number. Since an individual life has no intrinsic value, whether this is viewed from the perspective of the totalitarian state or the totalitarian individual, the decision is made on the basis of how much it will benefit the ones making the decision. And the greatest good will be determined on the basis of whatever maximizes pleasure and minimizes pain. By this calculus whatever is defective has no value at all since it will be less useful than a whole and healthy life and will certainly engender less pleasure, since society will have to utilize its resources for its benefit without getting any material benefit in return.

The Christian vision found in the teaching of Saint Josemaria is thoroughly different from this. Life has an intrinsic value, not by virtue of what it can do or contribute, but by virtue of what it *is*, a reflection of that from whom all blessings flow, from whom all life is drawn, from whom all goodness proceeds. The human person is the precious child of the all-powerful, all-loving Father God.

A deep awareness of the divine source of all human existence and of the Christian's participation in the divine nature not only leads to growth in personal holiness, but has profound social and cultural consequences as well. At the beginning of this week we celebrated Epiphany, the Feast of the Three Kings. When St. Josemaria reflected on the implications of Christ's revelation to the Gentiles through the visit of the three kings, he saw its importance for all humanity. Every human soul is of infinite value because of its source and its end, God Himself. On the Feast of the Epiphany Josemaria preached: "We Christians cannot exclude anyone; we cannot segregate or classify souls. 'Many will come from the East and West.' (Mt. 8:11) All find a place in Christ's heart. His arms, as we admire him again in the manger, are those of a child; but they are the same arms that will be extended on the cross drawing all men to himself."[7]

When Josemaria says we cannot "segregate or classify souls" he was surely thinking of the various races and classes of men on the face of the earth, but the implication of his teaching extends to those we do not usually consider. We also cannot place into a class of less value those who are unborn, those who are in a persistent vegetative state, those who dying, those who are disabled. We cannot "segregate or classify" those souls either, as though they were of less value than others. Each is a child of God and each carries a dignity as God's child which may never be violated.

Sometimes when we see the pervasive character of what Pope John Paul II has called the Culture of Death we can almost despair. The wealthier nations attempt to impose abortion as a human right on any nation, such as Ireland,

[7]*Christ is Passing By*, 65.

which has the courage to try to maintain constitutional protection for the unborn. The United Nations, the United States, and organizations such as Planned Parenthood expend literally billions of dollars to advance an agenda that will segregate, classify, and destroy souls which they absurdly see as threats. The Pope himself acknowledges the temptation to despair in his great encyclical, *The Gospel of Life*: "Humanity today offers us a truly alarming spectacle, if we consider not only how extensively attacks on life are spreading but also their unheard-of numerical proportion, and the fact that they receive widespread and powerful support from a broad consensus on the part of society, from widespread legal approval and the involvement of certain sectors of health-care personnel."[8] He even goes so far as to say that it looks as though goodness cannot prevail in the face of such evil. "Faced with the countless grave threats to life present in the modern world, one could feel overwhelmed by sheer powerlessness: good can never be powerful enough to triumph over evil!."[9]

But St. Josemaria speaks directly to this temptation to despair. He speaks about hope and cheerfulness to those people of good will in the world today fighting for the dignity of all human life when they might feel overwhelmed by these threats. "Cheerfulness is a necessary consequence of our divine filiation, of knowing that our Father God loves us with a love of predilection, that he holds us up and helps us and forgives us. Remember this and never forget it: even if it should seem at times that everything around you is collapsing, in fact nothing is collapsing at all, because God does not lose battles."[10]

It is the nature of love to be expansive, to be life generative. Those who love, love life. This is why those who love their spouses are naturally open to the gift of life. A loving society will be a fruitful society. St. Josemaria would be unspeakably pained to know that the land of his birth, Spain, and his adopted land, Italy, home to the Holy See, now have the lowest birth rates in the world. These societies do violence to themselves by not having the love which of its nature leads to life.

The life engendering nature of human love is what makes it reflective of divine love. St. Josemaria loved fertility – of God, if you will, of married couples, of the apostolate. When he visited Brazil in 1974 he loved hearing a story which was supposed to be reflective of the love, and hence the fertility, of the Brazilian people. He was told of the goal posts which were planted in a soccer field and then began to sprout.

When he addressed the Brazilians, he likened their country to a fertile, loving mother.

Brazil! The first thing I have found here is a mother: big, beautiful, fruitful and gentle, opening her arms to all, without distinction of language, race or nation, and who calls them all her children. . . . There is a lot, a lot to be done

---

[8] *The Gospel of Life*, 17.
[9] *The Gospel of Life*, 29.
[10] *The Forge*, 332.

here. . . . So, get moving! Multiply yourselves and do many good things in this land which is so fruitful.[11]

That same exhortation could be delivered to every nation on earth. It is love which is fruitful, and only love. Indeed, the most pure of all human loves was so fruitful that it led to a Virgin conceiving life.

It is easy to become discouraged in our struggle for the dignity of the human person in our day. But our sense of divine filiation will give us the fortitude, patience, and cheerfulness that we need to carry on the struggle, not in a half-hearted way but with real enthusiasm and zeal.

In realizing that we are the children of God we take courage in the fact that we have Mary as our Mother. As Blessed Josemaria told us with great simplicity: "Here is a piece of advice I shall never tire of telling souls: Love the Mother of God madly, for she is our Mother too."[12] And she is the Mother who bore the Word of Life, He Who took our humanity of her flesh, Who joined Himself with all humanity, even embryonic humanity. She is a powerful intercessor on behalf of those who are weak and vulnerable and at the margins of society. Under the kingship of Christ and through the intercession of the Blessed Virgin and our beloved Josemaria, we can each make our essential and unique contribution to a future civilization of love and life.

---

[11] Salvador Bernal, *A Profile of Msgr. Escriva, Founder of Opus Dei,* London, 1977, p. 231.

[12] *The Forge,* 77.

JOSÉ LUIS SORIA

SAINT JOSEMARIA ESCRIVA, A PORTRAIT

Introduction

It happens with literary portraits as it does with photographic, sculpted, or painted ones. A person can be described by words in many different manners, depending on the skills, the psychology, and the moods of the artist, but any good portrait demands a lot from the author: in fact not every painter or sculptor is necessarily a good portraitist. It is said that any outstanding painted portrait must take up the challenge to render life without aid of the spoken or the written word. One Dutch poet, commenting on the famous portrait of Cornelis Anslo—a renowned preacher—by Rembrandt said: "That's right, Rembrandt paints Cornelis's voice! His visible self is a second choice. The invisible can only be known through the word. For Anslo to be seen, he must be heard."

A portrait (not *the* portrait) of Saint Josemaria Escriva is my task today. My credentials as painter are non-existent, but my credentials for attempting a literary portrait of the founder of Opus Dei are the 22 years I spent very close to him, in Rome, from 1953 to the very day of his death in June 26, 1975. That day, as his family physician during the last years of his life, I tried to resuscitate him after he suffered a massive heart attack in the room where his two successive successors at the head of Opus Dei and myself were with him. After one hour and a half of vain efforts by a small group involved in the task, some of them also physicians, I closed his eyes with my fingers.

Painters make frequent use of sketches in their work. In a conventional sketch, the emphasis usually is laid on the general design and composition of the work and on its overall feeling, and there are three main types of functional sketches. The first—sometimes known as a *croquis*—is intended to remind the artist of some scene or event he has seen and wishes to record in a more permanent form. The second type is related to portraiture and notes the look on a face, the turn of a head, or other physical characteristics of a prospective sitter. The third—a *pochade*—is one in which he records, usually in color, the atmospheric effects and general impressions of a landscape. Today it is my task to present to you sketches of the first two types (the *croquis* and the notes I keep in my memory from the first time I met Saint Josemaria and the following few years), plus a more complete portrait based in the other twenty years I worked and lived close to him. John Coverdale will take care of the *pochade*, describing for us the times and the historical scenario of Saint Josemaria's life and work.

First sketch or the first impressions

When I met the now Saint Josemaria in the fall of 1953, the central point attracting my attention was that I was meeting the founder of Opus Dei. I knew, too, that the founders of most institutions in the Church had been beatified or canonized. Usually when the Lord places on the shoulders of a man or a woman the task of opening a new way in the following of Christ, He chooses the appropriate instrument. Whatever the difficulties such a foundation will meet (and the founding of Opus Dei implied incredible difficulties of all kinds) the founder or foundress is given the necessary graces to be faithful to the mission received. I knew very little more about the then Monsignor Escriva and, even in connection with his physical aspect, my knowledge was extremely limited since previous to that day in 1953 I remembered having seen only one picture of him, taken probably 13 or 14 years earlier.

Of course, never before in my life had I been acquainted with a personality such as Saint Josemaria, but I was not overwhelmed. In the years to come I was going to have the opportunity of hearing the question he addressed sometimes to young members of Opus Dei when they arrived in Rome: "How did you imagine the Father? As a stern, solemn and serious character?" In fact he was for us (young professionals or university students at the time) the incarnation of a loving, cheerful, amusing and strong father. It was so easy to love him! The get-togethers we had with him were sheer pleasure: good humor, sometimes to the point of explosive laughter, and at the same time incredible occasions of learning about God, the characteristics of the spirit of Opus Dei, the history of the Church, funny or interesting anecdotes based on art and literature, news about the apostolic activities of Opus Dei in other countries, etc. Close to two hundred people were then crammed into the headquarters of Opus Dei, which were under construction, some parts already finished in a Roman traditional style, and some parts of the pre-existing buildings awaiting demolition. I remember Saint Josemaria teasing one young man from the United States about one of the parts recently finished, but giving the appearance of almost a venerable age, due to the skills of Roman painters and construction workers. The *patina* fooled the person who was questioned, who declared himself convinced that that part should not survive the demolition: it was "too old"!

His immense, enormous faith and, as a consequence, his unity of life, without independent compartments separating prayer and action, was another trait of his personality, immediately evident after meeting him. Saint Josemaria had suffered and would continue to suffer because some people (many of whom should have known better) interpreted his faith as fanaticism or madness. But for me, and also for many other people, this was an outstanding characteristic of the founder, quite different from the Sunday Catholics, including some "Sunday priests", I had know before.

I will always remember the impression I received when in the summer of 1950 I had the opportunity of hearing a tape, in which a meditation on Faith preached by Saint Josemaria in 1947 was recorded. Years later he was going to rework it and publish it in *Friends of God,*[1] with the title "Living by Faith." But a similar impression was created every time I attended one of his preached meditations, and the occasions were many to say the least. His words were very powerful, simple and deep, attractive and challenging, moving from the most delicate moments of dialogue with Jesus in the Blessed Sacrament or compassionate understanding of human weakness to instances of forceful and sometimes thunderous demands upon the listeners. It was mostly dialogue with the Lord, but certainly he knew how to teach us to share in the same dialogue.

Convinced of his sanctity and future canonization, from the very moment I had the opportunity I kept as souvenirs or relics everything I could obtain. I remember among those things an empty bottle of insulin—the strong diabetes suffered by Saint Josemaria until April 1954 forced him to receive large doses; a rosary he blessed and gave me; several small papers with some of his hand writing... But my stay in Rome was going to be much longer that I had initially planed. In fact my original idea was that, after three years of ecclesiastical studies and formation in the spirit of Opus Dei, I was going to return to my native Spain to pursue my career as a physician. The prayers, the example, and the preaching of Saint Josemaria changed all that, and led me to the priesthood. Once I was ordained in 1956, the founder wanted me to remain in Rome, working close to him, and there I stayed for twenty more years. Nineteen of those twenty years allow me today to attempt a passage from the sketch to a portrait of the founder of Opus Dei.

A full portrait

Fifteenth-century portraits, by Pisanello or Jan van Eyck, for example, may be considered completed pictorial works in their concentration, execution, and distribution of space. The clear, delicately delineated representation follows every detail of the surface, striving for realism. The profile, rich in detail, is preferred; resembling relief, it is akin to the medallion. More interested in the psychological aspects of portraiture, late 19th- and 20th-century draftsmen prefer the softer crayons that readily follow every artistic impulse. Mood elements, intellectual tension, and personal engagement are typical features of the modern portrait and thus also of modern portrait drawing. In my attempt as a portraitist I will be eclectic, even if incomplete, but I should start with a point that gives reason for all the other details of my sitter.

As the late Bishop Alvaro del Portillo, the first successor of Saint Josemaria at the head of Opus Dei, put it, "To understand the character of our founder, one must keep in view this basic quality which pervaded everything else: his dedication to God, and to all souls for God's sake; his constant readiness to correspond generously to the will of God. This was the aim of his whole life. He was a man in love, a man possessed of a secret he would later spell out

---

[1] First published in English in 1981, *Friends of God* is a translation of *Amigos de Dios*, Madrid, 1977.

in point No. 1006 of *The Forge:* "With crystal clarity I see the formula, the secret of happiness, both earthly and eternal. It is not just a matter of accepting the will of God, but of embracing it, of identifying oneself with it—in a word, of loving the divine will with a positive act of our own will. This, I repeat, is the infallible secret of joy and peace."[2]

Character strength was one of his outstanding dimensions. "He was endowed with a keen, agile intellect that was complemented by a lively interest in all branches of knowledge, by a remarkable juridical mentality, and by a most refined aesthetic sense. His personality was vibrant and vigorous; his temperament was courageous and impetuous, strong and energetic; and he managed to acquire a remarkable degree of self-mastery."[3] I must say that the strongest correction I have received during my adult life came from Saint Josemaria, as a consequence of my negligence in a particular set of circumstances. But not even then did I feel less loved. He had the gift of showing his authentic affection especially when he feared that his words or deeds could have hurt the feelings of some of us. He was an open and sometimes even blunt man who disliked ceremony and façade. He loved sincerity and personal freedom. His strong character and temper were softened by a keen sense of humor and a smile that would light up his face and make his penetrating eyes sparkle. Yes, as the Postulator of his Cause of Canonization put it recently, "he had an iron will and very great gentleness. He asked for high and demanding goals, but he was able to motivate with his charity .... He did not ask the impossible."

He was obviously a man totally dedicated to serving the Church, despite all obstacles, according to the charism received (the founding of Opus Dei). Probably this was the reason why, referring to this love for the Church, he used to add that his goal was "to serve the Church as the Church wants to be served," not—I would add—as the limitations of an inappropriate canonical frame would impose or as the opinion of some members of the clergy would prefer.

He was magnanimous, especially in everything related to the divine worship, but also in the care he took of the duties of friendship and hospitality. I remember that the first time I heard the name "Chateauneuf-du-Pape" (the renowned brand of French wine) was on the occasion of Christmas gifts he was sending to some friends in the Vatican Curia, at a time of serious financial straits.

His artistic good taste was outstanding. His literary style was very good. I must say with deep gratitude that the greatest source of my education in those fields comes from his influence and example. His heart—maternal and paternal at the same time—and his immense love for God enriched him with leadership and energy, yes, but also with a tremendous warmth and humanity. When I first arrived in the Eternal City, he somehow found out that my father wasn't entirely pleased with my decision to study in Rome for few years. Saint Josemaria urged me to write home often, to pray and be confident that things

[2]Alvaro del Portillo, in *Immersed in God*, Princeton, N.J., 1996, p. 31-32.
[3]*Ibid.* p. 33.

would change. The strategy worked and my father eventually became a Cooperator of Opus Dei. When I was ordained in 1956, he donated a beautiful chalice that the late Alvaro del Portillo used at Mass for several years.

Some of my most touching memories of Saint Josemaria's kindness involve the death of my parents. It is easy to understand that these paint strokes are noticeable in my portrait. Early in 1967, my mother underwent surgery... only to be sewn up again because the cancer was too far advanced. She was a member of Opus Dei and had had the opportunity of meeting Saint Josemaria during one of his trips to Spain. The founder often asked about her and he told me that he kept her in his prayers. I once mentioned to him that I hadn't heard any news for several weeks and he told me to phone home right away. But other duties distracted me and the day slipped away.

The next morning, he asked me again about my mother. When he learned that I hadn't called the hospital where she was staying, he reprimanded me in no uncertain terms and he told me to do so that very day. That afternoon I got through and was able to talk to both my mother and my father. It was the last time I heard her voice. She died suddenly on Good Friday, a few weeks later. When I was leaving for her funeral, the Father blessed me, hugged me, and whispered in my ear: "Son, I have gone through the same thing myself." He was referring to the unexpected death of his mother in 1941, while he was away from Madrid preaching a retreat to priests of another diocese.

When I returned to Rome he asked first about my father. Then he told me that a letter from my mother had arrived during my absence. He was referring to a letter she had dictated to one of my sisters two days before she died. "Don't read it today; you will only cry your eyes out," he advised. "Wait a week; then read it and keep it. It will be a real treasure for you."

Early in 1973, my father's health began to fail. Several times the doctors predicted that the end was near and Saint Josemaria would send me home to Spain. But each time my father would recover and I would head back to Rome. Just before the summer, Saint Josemaria—as was customary of him—told his closest collaborators to take a few weeks to rest and lend a hand in the apostolic activities of Opus Dei in whatever European country they wished – with one exception. Turning to me, he said: "You'll go to Spain. That way you can be with your father." And while I was in Spain, my father's health took a sudden turn for the worse. I was able to be with him at the end, prepare him for death, and administer the last rites of the Church.

Peter Berglar, one of his biographers, wrote that "to his very last day, [the founder's] face retained a youthful, boyish expression. This was partly due to his soft features –the rounded chin, the full cheeks- and the simple parting of his short, slowly graying hair. Mostly, however, it was his smile." In those pictures—I want to point out that Berglar's comments referred obviously to the pictures he had seen—"the same smile plays about his mouth and eyes: a smile full of warmth, amusement, and unaffected concern, yet without any shadow of anxiety. His was a face without any trace of bitterness or ennui; it was transparently guileless, candid, cheerfully interested." The German historian adds:

"[his face] was not a scarred battle field where elation and sorrow, God and the devil had waged war; it was not a dramatic stage." "That is why his portraits are not as fascinating as Beethoven's or Einstein's", he comments.[4] And there I disagree with Berglar.

St.Josemaria at Fatima, Portugal, November 2, 1972.

It is true that most photographs of Saint Josemaria match the charming description made by the German biographer, but not all of them. There is a different group of photographs of the founder of Opus Dei, which Berglar has not seen or forgets. I am referring to the type of photographs I would dare call *transcendent* or *pictures on the way of the Cross*. All of them have as common background an intense and actual physical, spiritual, or moral suffering when the photograph was taken. As an example of these *transcendent* pictures I would mention the one taken during the Spanish Civil war for the documents from the Honduras embassy, where Josemaria Escriva appears in civil attire, documents that allowed him to continue carrying out his pastoral ministry often in the street and at the risk of his life in the midst of a cruel religious persecution; or the photograph taken also in Madrid on March 28, 1939, at the end of the war, while he is inspecting the rubble of the first and only Student Residence that Opus Dei had promoted; or the ones taken in Fatima in 1972, in Lujan (Argentina) in 1974, and in Torreciudad in 1975 praying the Rosary during his Marian pilgrimages for the needs of the Church. The last picture taken during his life belongs to this group as well, where we see him in Villa delle Rose, Castelgandolfo, one hour and a half before his death.

All these pictures reflect a very deep and typical trait of Saint Josemaria: he was a man marked by the Cross, but not made unhappy or miserable by the sufferings he endured. A privileged way of knowing the intimate characteristics of his are the Personal Notes or *Apuntes íntimos* (a set of notes of a confidential nature written mostly in the 1930's and that the founder specified were not to be read until after his death). The entry for September 14, 1931 reads:

[4]Peter Berglar, *Opus Dei. Life and Work of his Founder Josemaría Escrivá,* Princeton, N.J., 1993, p. 271.

"Feast of the Exaltation of the Holy Cross, 1931: How much today's epistle cheered me up! In it the Holy Spirit, through Saint Paul, teaches the secret of immortality and glory... This is the sure path: through humiliation, to the cross; and from the cross, with Christ, to the immortal glory of the Father."[5] In a homily on October 2, 1968, the fortieth anniversary of the founding of Opus Dei, he said: "If at that moment [October 1928] I had seen what was awaiting me, I would have died, so great is the weight of what I have had to suffer and enjoy!". And he repeated many, many times another thought he recorded in *Furrow*, 257, as well: "The Lord, the Eternal Priest, always blesses with the Cross."[6]

From early childhood to the last day of his life, the cross was his constant companion. In important issues related to the founding and development of Opus Dei, or to the situation of the Church in general, or in minute details of domestic daily life. I remember that, for many years, those of us living with him used to joke about the action of what we called the "plumber devil," because by accident, coincidence or Providence many feast days or happy anniversaries that were supposed to be occasions for joy and relaxation were transformed into hectic, tense moments by the unexpected rupture of a drain, the leaking of a pipe, the bursting of a radiator in the most upsetting place or moment, literally as if somebody wanted to water down the serenity of the feast day. But it was in vain. In 1931 Saint Josemaria had learned the lesson very well: "Generally, Jesus gives me a cross with joy, *cum gaudio et pace* [with joy and peace]; and a cross with joy... is not a cross. Given my optimistic nature, I have habitually a joy that we might call physiological—that of a healthy animal. It is not to that joy that I am referring, but to another, a supernatural kind which comes from abandoning oneself and everything else into the loving arms of God our Father."[7]

A supernatural episode during his Mass on February 14, 1943 was often defined by Saint Josemaria as the moment when God wanted "to crown his Work with the Holy Cross." It was then that the founder received inspirational light to find a juridical path for the priestly ordination of the priests in the Work, and it was also the occasion for the inclusion of the name of the Cross in the title and seal of Opus Dei, up to the present day and always: *Prelature of the Holy Cross and Opus Dei*. Always the Cross!

In my office I keep two pictures of Saint Josemaria. One of them, in color, the one chosen for the tapestry in Saint Peter's balcony the day of his Beatification, is the paradigm of the type of photographs described by Dr. Berglar. The other, in black and white and taken, I think, in 1970, is for me the model of the *transcendent* portraits of Saint Josemaria. In that picture the founder is serious, even if you can guess that at any moment he could insinu-

---

[5] *Apuntes íntimos,* no. 284 in Andrés Vázquez de Prada, *The Founder of Opus Dei: The Life of Josemaria Escrivá,* vol. I: *The early Years*, Princeton, N.J., 2001, p. 293.

[6] *Furrow,* 257.

[7] *Apuntes íntimos*, no. 350, in *The Founder of Opus Dei...*, page 302.

ate a smile of love and sympathy. He looks very, very intently at the camera, and therefore at you when you study the picture. His eyes, underlined by dark rings, are deep behind the bifocals. The hair is a little bit in disarray and the wrinkles and flaccid skin in the neck talk of many years spent in dedication and service. To me—prompted by Berglar's remarks—this picture is much more inspiring and meaningful than any portrait of Beethoven or Einstein and it completes very well the image conveyed by the other type of photograph. I love them both—the one full of light and the other full of intensity—because they provide me with a complete set of the most striking memories of the years I spent close to Saint Josemaria: joy and good humor, as a consequence of his temperament but also as a result of his certainty of being a child of God. And intense and almost constant suffering, also as the proof of his identification with the crucified Christ, in a "co-redemption of Love" based in his own active and passive self-denial.[8] Last September, on the feast day of the Triumph of the Cross, John Paul II said that "the cross is the supreme symbol of love." Saint Josemaria was the greatest man I have ever known and worked with, but he was not superman. His soul was extremely sensitive to suffering, even if he knew how to love and to unite his sufferings with the redemptive sufferings of Christ. I heard him say many times that true joy has its roots in the shape of a cross. That is why his best portrait probably is the one he himself painted, when for many years he wrote in the first page of the liturgical calendar: "*In laetitia, nulla dies sine cruce. In joy, no day without the cross.*"

---

[8]Cf. *Furrow*, no. 255.

JOHN F. COVERDALE

SAINT JOSEMARIA ESCRIVA AND
THE ANTICLERICALISM OF THE EARLY
SECOND REPUBLIC[1]

St. Josemaria Escriva, whom I will refer to in this paper as Escriva, often described himself as "anticlerical" because his exalted conception of the priesthood led him to reject its use for temporal ends, and because his appreciation for the autonomy of the lay members of the Church led him to reject efforts by the clergy to dictate to them in areas that properly belong to their free choice. During the Second Spanish Republic (1931-39), however, he faced an anticlericalism entirely different from his own. This paper will focus on Escriva's experience of that anticlericalism during the early years of the Second Republic rather than during the Civil War and the years immediately preceding it.

The anticlericalism Escriva faced during this period found expression in an atmosphere of hostility to the Church and particularly to priests and religious, in legislation designed to eliminate or at least lessen the Church's influence in the public life of the country, and in violent attacks on church property and on priests and religious.

The Roots of Anticlericalism in Spanish History

This type of anticlericalism had deep roots in Spanish history.[2] From the early 1800s, middle class liberals, whose political ideology was rooted in the French Enlightenment, struggled to reduce the influence and power of the Church in Spain. In the period between 1830 and 1860, liberal governments confiscated large amounts of Church-owned land that had been used to support the clergy and the members of religious orders. The confiscation of the Church's property made the clergy dependent on the inadequate stipends which the government agreed to pay in partial compensation for the confiscated property.

---

[1] Published with the permission of the Pontifical University of the Holy Cross.

[2] Extensive background in W. Callahan, *Church, Politics, and Society in Spain, 1750-1874*, Cambridge, Mass. 1984, and *The Catholic Church in Spain, 1875-1998*, Washington, D.C., 2000. Selected documents in M. Revuelta Gonzalez, *El Anticlericalismo español en sus documentos*, Barcelona, 1999.

Anticlericalism was tightly interwoven with political, economic, cultural and social developments. *Cf.* J. R. Montero Gibert, "La CEDA y la Iglesia en la Segunda República Española," *Revista de Estudios Políticos*, Nueva Epoca, 31-32 (1983), pp. 103-104. Limitations of space, however, force me to treat it largely as if it were a free-standing phenomenon.

During the conservative resurgence that began in 1876 and continued up to Spain's humiliating defeat in the Spanish-American War of 1898, the Church regained some of its social position and influence, although not its property. The Church also flourished internally, with a new growth of fervor and an increase in vocations to the priesthood and religious life.

The period was marked by tension over religious issues. Fervent Catholics saw society and religion endangered by the advance of a secular wave of liberal free-thinkers and Masons. Many considered liberalism a heresy and rejected altogether the constitutional parliamentary monarchy. Others accepted the constitutional regime as a lesser evil, but yearned for a fully confessional state that would enforce Catholic unity. To liberals, the resurgence of the Church meant handing Spain over to the enemy of modern institutions and allowing the forces of the past to direct society.

Spain's disastrous defeat in the Spanish-American War moved Spaniards of all political persuasions to seek ways to "regenerate" the country. Conservatives focused on reform of political institutions. Middle class liberals and radicals sought to transform not merely politics but the entire society. They strove to reduce or eliminate the role of the Church in Spanish life, especially in education.

Among the working class, socialists saw the Church as a mainstay of the existing economic order that needed to be rooted out, but economic revolution was much more important to them than attacking the Church directly.[3] Anarchists, by contrast, aimed to create above all a new morality and a new culture. The elimination of religion would be a defining feature of the new order they hoped to inaugurate. For them, opposition to the Church, and more generally to religion, was not merely something that would facilitate economic revolution, but a vital component of a new way of life.[4]

Anticlericalism turned violent during the Tragic Week in Barcelona in July 1909.[5] Massive draft riots, triggered by a decision to mobilize reserve units after a Spanish defeat in north Africa, led to the burning of monasteries,

[3]In 1902 the Spanish Socialist leader Pablo Iglesias wrote: "[T]he principal enemy is not clericalism but capitalism. ... This does not mean that socialists will not do everything they can to oppose the preponderance of clericalism, which has become —more or less voluntarily depending on the country— a powerful ally of the exploiting classes." Quoted in V. Arbeloa, *Socialismo y Anticlericalismo*, Madrid, 1973, p. 158.

[4]*See* S. Payne, *Spanish Catholicism,* Madison, 1984, pp. 125-126.

[5]There had been important outbreaks of anti-clerical violence in the past. The most important occurred in 1834 when rumors ran through Madrid that Jesuits and groups of friars had caused a cholera epidemic among the poor by poisoning the public water supply to punish the capital for its impiety. Between fifty and one hundred priests and monks lost their lives in the riots that ensued. The propaganda that triggered the riots was similar in tone and psychology to the crude anti-Semitism that routinely spread, in many parts of Europe, stories of ritual murders of children by Jews. Middle class anticlerical propagandists from Masonic lodges and other secret societies that were a powerful force among Spanish liberals probably originated much of this propaganda. The fact that urban mobs believed the rumors and acted upon them, however, suggests that by the early nineteenth century a significant number of workers were already sufficiently

convents and schools and the profaning of tombs and religious images. By the time the riots had been put down, twenty-one of Barcelona's fifty-eight churches, thirty of its seventy-five convents and monasteries, and some thirty other church-related schools and buildings used for social services had gone up in flames. There were also numerous incidents of desecration of sacred objects and violation of tombs of religious. Two clergymen were murdered by rioters and another perished in a fire set by them.[6]

The violent anti-clerical propaganda that had been spread in Barcelona by Radical Republicans for a number of years undoubtedly played some part in the events of the Tragic Week, but it is still far from clear why draft riots gave rise to widespread attacks on Church property and desecration of religious objects. Whatever their cause, the Barcelona riots confirmed that sizeable numbers of urban workers had not only grown disaffected from the Church but had become violently hostile towards it.

During the next two decades there were no major outbreaks of anticlerical violence, although propaganda against the Church continued. The support prominent Catholics offered to the Primo de Rivera dictatorship deepened the conviction of many Republicans and other liberals that the Church was a major obstacle to their desires for reform. During the Primo de Rivera dictatorship and the interlude that followed it, however, anticlerical forces were held in check by the government which prevented them from taking any overt action against the Church.

The Beginning of the Second Republic

In 1931, the monarchy was replaced by the Second Republic. Significant numbers of Catholics, especially in the larger cities, had voted for Republican candidates in the elections that led to the proclamation of the Second Republic, and many other Catholics were willing to give the new regime a chance. The provisional coalition government was headed by a Catholic and two other Catholics formed part of it. Most of the ministers of the new government were, however, more or less openly anti-Catholic. For them, the Republic represented not merely a different form of government, but a different, radically secular, vision of life and society.[7] One of the provisional government's first measures was a declaration of religious freedom and the separation of church and state, although it assured Catholics that it would not persecute any religion.[8]

---

disaffected from the Church to be open to such crude propaganda. S. Payne, *Spanish Catholicism*, p. 82. See also A. Moliner Prada, "El anticlericalismo popular durante el bienio 1834-1835," *Hispania Sacra* 49 (1997), pp. 497-541.

[6] J. Ullman, *The Tragic Week: A Study of Anticlericalism in Spain 1875-1912,* Cambridge, Mass., 1968.

[7] M. Álvarez Tardío, Fray Lazo: *El anticlericalismo radical ante el debate constituyente de la Segunda República Española (1931),* Hispania Sacra 50 (1998), p. 251- 273.

[8] J.M. Sánchez, *Reform and Reaction: The Politico-Religious Background of the Spanish Civil War,* Chapel Hill, 1964, p. 74.

Few Catholics welcomed the proclamation of religious freedom or the proposal to disestablish the Church, but the initial reaction both of the Catholic rank and file and of the hierarchy was restrained. The majority continued to accept the new regime, with misgivings but without overtly hostile acts. In a letter to the Nuncio, the Vatican Secretary of State, Cardinal Pacelli, urged Catholics not to give importance to the question of monarchy versus republic but to concentrate on the defense of social order and the rights of the Church. The Nuncio, in his turn, exhorted Catholics, and particularly the bishops, to accept the new regime and to remain united in defense of the Church.[9] The first sign of overt hostility of some members of the hierarchy toward the new regime came on May 1, 1931 when the Archbishop of Toledo and Primate of Spain, Cardinal Segura, published a pastoral letter praising the king.

On May 10, 1931, the playing of the monarchist hymn at a royalist club in Madrid provoked an attack by supporters of the republic that soon degenerated into three days of violence directed primarily against churches, monasteries and convents. Rioting soon spread from Madrid to other cities.

The provisional republican government did not provoke the burning of the convents, but it was very slow to react to the violence, at least partly because many of its members were more or less sympathetic to the rioters.[10] Manuel Azaña, who was rapidly becoming the most powerful political figure in the country, told his colleagues that "all the convents of Madrid are not worth the life of a single Republican;" and threatened to resign "if a single person is injured in Madrid because of this stupidity."[11] For several days, the government did nothing to control the riots. Once it did intervene, the violence ended quickly, but by that time approximately one hundred churches and convents had been burnt throughout Spain, including forty-one in Malaga.[12] The government's inaction during the early days of the rioting convinced Catholics throughout the country that the new regime was an implacable enemy of the Church.

Anticlerical Legislation of the Provisional Government

The sense of the Republic's hostility to the Church soon increased as the provisional government issued a series of decrees and regulations that upset many Catholics. It established full freedom of conscience and cult, made religious instruction voluntary in state schools, dissolved the chaplain corps of the army

---

[9]A. Fernández García, *La iglesia ante el establecimiento de la II República,* "Cuadernos de Historia Moderna y Contemporaneous" 5 (1984), pp. 215-37.

[10]J. De La Cueva Merino, *El Anticlericalismo en la Segunda República y la Guerra Civil,* in E. La Parra López and M. Suárez Cortina (Eds.), *El Anticlericalismo español contemporáneo,* Madrid 1998, p. 221.

[11]S. Payne, *Spain's First Democracy. The Second Republic 1931-1936,* Madison, 1993, p. 44-46.

[12]Escriva was especially affected by the violence in Malaga since Isidoro Zorzano was living there at the time. For a detailed account of events in Malaga, A. Garcia Sánchez, *La Segunda República en Málaga,* Cordoba, 1984, pp. 227-288.

and navy, substituted a promise for the traditional oath of office, deprived the Church of representation in the National Council on Education, and prohibited government officials from attending public religious acts. In a tolerant, religiously pluralistic society, many of these actions would seem acceptable. Most Spanish Catholics, reared in a society in which a large majority of the population was at least nominally Catholic and in which close cooperation between church and state had been the norm for centuries, viewed all of them as hostile to the Church.[13] Their sense of hostility was increased by the government's failure to negotiate with or even consult Church officials about changes in religious policy, despite a long tradition of handling religious affairs through treaties with the Holy See.

In May, 1931, the government expelled the bishop of Vitoria. The next month it expelled Cardinal Segura, the highest ranking churchman in Spain, for anti-Republican statements and attitudes. Although both bishops had given Republican officials good grounds for considering them opponents of the new regime, their expulsion confirmed the conviction of many Catholics that the new government was an enemy of the Church.

The Constituent Assembly and the Constitution

In the elections for a constituent assembly in summer 1931, Catholics and conservatives were in disarray. They ran a strong second in many areas, but won only a small number of seats because the winner-take-all electoral law awarded each seat to the party that won the district.[14]

Parties hostile to the Church had an overwhelming majority in the constituent assembly. They were not interested in a bloody persecution like that going on at the time in Mexico or the Soviet Union, but their goals went well beyond turning Spain into a non-confessional country. They wanted it to become a modern society, and in their minds, this meant a society in which religion might play a role in the individual lives of some people but would be absent from public life.

In light of their secularized vision of modernity, it is understandable that Republican leaders considered the Church, and particularly the religious orders that were so influential in Spanish education, the major obstacle to their plans

---

[13]It was not only on the Catholic side that these measures were viewed as hostile to the Church. Many of their liberal proponents championed them precisely as ways of attacking the Church. In Spain in the 1930s, most people saw the only choices as laicism or a confessional state. Few people could conceive of a non-confessional state that respected religion and the church. M. D. Gómez Molleda, "Massoneria e anticlericalismo nella Spagna del XX secolo," in A. Mola, *Stato, Chiesa e Società in Italia, Francia, Belgio e Spagna nei secoli XIX-XX,* Foggia 1993, p. 311.

[14]V. Cárcel Ortí, "La II República y la Guerra Civil (1931-39)," in *Historia de la Iglesia en España,* t. V, Madrid, 1989, 330. This electoral system, which is similar to the one used in the United States, gives parties that may garner a large number of votes nationwide but fail to win a majority in many districts much less voice in government than systems of proportional representation.

for modernizing Spain. In order to reduce the Church's influence on society, they were bent on abolishing the Jesuits and restricting the activities of other religious orders. Above all, they were determined to eliminate Catholic influence in education by prohibiting priests and religious from running schools.

Like the changes already introduced by the Provisional Government, all of these goals struck most Spanish Catholics, many of whom drew no distinctions between their religious faith and their social and cultural traditionalism, as unjustified attacks on religion.

The Spanish bishops initially limited themselves to exhorting Spanish Catholics to accept peacefully the legitimate decrees of the government and to remain united. In August, however, they prepared a collective pastoral letter criticizing not only the proposed provisions of the constitution but also "the so called 'modern' freedoms that are considered the most precious conquest of the French Revolution and the untouchable patrimony of the democracies hostile to the Church."[15] The moderate members of the hierarchy and the Papal Nuncio considered the document inopportune, but the intransigent faction, headed by the Cardinal of Toledo, insisted successfully on its publication.

The draft constitution prepared by the constituent assembly during summer and fall 1931 contained a number of provisions that directly affected the Church. The first important measure to be approved, Article 3, put an end to the union of Church and State that had characterized Spain for centuries. "The State," Article 3 declared, "has no official religion."[16]

On October 14, 1931 the Assembly approved what would become Article 26 of the Constitution, the principal provision dealing with Church affairs. It forbade the central, regional and local governments from favoring or supporting the Church in any way. Specifically, it called for eliminating within two years the subsidies the government had been paying to the clergy since it had had confiscated Church property in the nineteenth century.

The most important provisions of Article 26 affected the religious orders. An early draft had called for dissolution of all religious orders. The measure approved by the assembly did not go that far, but it did provide for the dissolution of the Jesuits and the confiscation of all their property. Other orders were subject to the threat of dissolution if the government felt their activities were a danger to the security of the state. In addition, religious orders were forbidden to own any property beyond what was strictly necessary for the maintenance of their members and the fulfillment of their specific aims.

The most damaging provision of Article 26 from the point of view of Spanish Catholics was one that forbade the orders that were permitted to continue working in Spain to engage in education. This sectarian provision demonstrates the determination of the anticlerical majority of the assembly to undermine the church at any cost. Spain was suffering from a desperate lack

---

[15]G. Redondo, *Historia de la Iglesia en España,* Madrid, 1993, Vol. I, p 146.

[16]*Idem,* p. 160, n. 7.

of schools, and the members of the assembly listed education among their top priorities. Yet they were attempting to force the closing of schools that were educating a substantial portion of the country's students because they hoped this would reduce the Church's influence in the country.[17]

Escriva's Personal Experience of Growing Anticlericalism

Professor Vázquez de Prada has given us a detailed treatment of Escriva's personal experiences of hostility toward priests and the Church in the early 1930s.[18] My account relies heavily on his.

When the mob began to attack churches and convents in Madrid on May 11, 1931, Escriva feared that the church of the Foundation for the Sick might be sacked and the Eucharist profaned. Dressed in borrowed lay clothes and accompanied by his younger brother, he slipped out the side door of the church "like a thief," carrying a ciborium full of consecrated hosts wrapped in a cassock and newspaper. As he hurried through the streets, he prayed with tears in his eyes, "Jesus, may each sacrilegious fire increase my fire of love and reparation!"[19] After depositing the Eucharist in the home of a friend, he observed in horror the smoke filling the sky of Madrid as churches and convents went up in flames.

On May 13, Escriva heard rumors that the Foundation for the Sick might soon be attacked. He hurriedly located a few rooms on Viriato Street and moved his family and their few belongings there. During the coming months, the family would crowd into a tiny apartment whose only windows were on an air shaft. Escriva's room was so small there was no room for a chair so he had to write kneeling down using the bed for a desk.

Escriva, who continued to wear his cassock on the street, as had been the custom in Spain, found himself increasingly the object of insults. In earlier years he had occasionally encountered hostility simply because he was a priest, but after the proclamation of the Republic, the insults became more frequent and more aggressive. In the midst of this hostile environment, he struggled to control his temper and to "pelt with Hail Marys,"[20] his attackers. He was not always successful.

During summer 1931, Escriva decided to make a novena to a recently deceased member of the Damas Apostolicas, Mercedes Reyna, visiting her tomb each day in a cemetery located in a poor neighborhood of Madrid. Every day of the novena brought with it new insults. Once on his way back from the cemetery, a bricklayer came at him shouting, "A cockroach! Step on it!"

---

[17]S. Payne, *Spanish Catholicism,* p. 156.

[18]A. Vásquez De Prada, *The Founder of Opus Dei. The Life of Josemaría Escriva,* Vol. I, *The Early Years,* Princeton, 2001. In many cases, I have translated directly from the Spanish. I will indicate where this happened with the annotation "Author's translation."

[19]*Idem,* p. 270.

[20]*Idem,* p. 275.

Despite his resolutions not to pay attention to such things, Escriva was unable to contain himself. "What courage," he retorted, "to pick a fight with someone who walks past without offending you!" The other workers told the bricklayer to shut up, and one of them tried to excuse his fellow worker's conduct. "It's not right," he said with the air of someone giving a satisfactory explanation, "but you have to understand, it's that he hates priests."[21]   Another day a boy shouted to his friends, "A priest! Let's throw stones at him!" Escriva recounts his reaction: "Without even thinking about it, I shut the breviary I had been reading, and faced them: 'You brats! Is that what your mothers teach you?'" "I added other words," he concludes, without specifying what they were.[22] On several occasions Escriva was hit by stones, and once a well-aimed soccer ball struck him full in the face.

By mid September, 1931 Escriva was able to record in his notes:

> I have to thank my God for a noteworthy change. Until recently the insults and jeers I received for being a priest (mostly since the coming of the Republic, before only rarely), made me angry. I made a resolution to entrust to Our Lady with a Hail Mary those from whom I heard vulgar and obscene expressions. I did it. It was hard. Now, when I hear that sort of ignoble words, I usually feel moved with pity, considering the misfortune of the poor people who do those things. They think they are doing something good, because people have taken advantage of their ignorance and passions to make them believe that priests are not only lazy parasites but their enemies, accomplices of the bourgeoisie that exploits them.[23]

Escriva finished his note with a characteristic exclamation that reflected his conviction that God intended to do great things through Opus Dei: "Your Work, Lord," he concluded, "will open their eyes!" [24]

Escriva's Reaction to Anticlerical Legislation

Escriva was saddened by the overtly anti-Catholic stance of many of the new leaders of the Second Republic and the harm they might do the Church. On April 20, 1931 he wrote in his personal notes:

> May the Immaculate Virgin defend our poor Spain and may God confound the enemies of our Mother the Catholic Church. The Spanish Republic. For 24 hours, Madrid was one huge mad house... Things seem to have calmed down. But the Masons do not sleep. ... The Heart of Jesus also keeps watch! This is my hope. How often these days, I have understood, I have heard the powerful cries of our Lord, that he loves his Work.[25]

When Escriva learned of the decree of dissolution of the Jesuits, he was

---

[21]*Idem,* p. 272. Author's translation.

[22]*Idem,* p. 271-272. Author's translation.

[23]*Idem,* Author's translation.

[24]*Idem.*

[25] *Idem,* p. 269. Author's translation. The reference in this text to the activity of Masons seems to indicate that Escriva attributed to Masonry much of the anticlericalism that was sweeping

deeply distressed. He wrote,

> Yesterday I suffered when I learned about the expulsion of the Jesuits and the other anti-Catholic measures adopted by the Parliament. My head ached and I felt sick until afternoon. In the afternoon, dressed as a layman, I went with Adolfo to Chamartin [where the Jesuits' house was located]. Fr. Sanchez and all the other Jesuits were delighted to suffer persecution [...] What serenely beautiful things he said to us![26]

Although Escriva was extremely concerned about attacks on the Church, he took no part in the debate raging among Spanish Catholics over how best to defend the Church. Many believed that the only way was to overturn the Second Republic and bring back the monarchy. Other Catholics argued that the form of government was not an essential matter. Catholics, they said, could and should work within the republican framework to protect the Church's rights.[27] Passions ran high on both sides of the debate. Opposing views were often taken as a sign of wrong headedness or a lack of zeal in the service of the Church.[28]

From his seminary days when he had been repelled by the clericalism that characterized large parts of the Spanish Church, Escriva had been convinced that priests should respect the right of lay Catholics to form their own political opinions and to join political parties of own their choice. He was also convinced that all Catholics should respect the choices of their fellow Catholics, even when they did not agree with them about how Catholic principles should be applied in a specific situation. Although he felt a lively interest in current events, because of these convictions he made it an inflexible rule throughout his life not to express his political opinions. This attitude was not merely a personal one. It was intimately connected to his role as the founder of Opus Dei.

In Spain, as well as in many other countries, Catholics in the first third of the twentieth century promoted many organizations whose purpose was to mobilize Catholics for political action to protect the Church's position in public life.[29] Opus Dei, which Escriva had founded less than three years before the proclamation of the Second Republic in Spain had different aims and goals. As

---

Spain. This inference finds support in other texts. It raises interesting questions about what other factors Escriva saw as the explanation of opposition to the Church in Spain. In the early 1930s, large parts of pastoral activities were in the poorest parts of Madrid. He was acutely aware of the misery that afflicted many, and understood that some of them saw the clergy as the allies of those who exploited them. (See text quoted above at note 22. His currently available writings do not indicate, however, whether he considered that their belief was in any way justified by the actions of members of the hierarchy and other Catholics. Nor do currently available texts permit drawing any conclusions about the extent to which Escriva attributed widespread hostility to the Church among middle class defenders of political, social and economic reform to their perception that the Church was a bulwark of conservatism.

[26] *Idem*, p. 274. Author's translation.

[27] S. Payne, *Spanish Catholicism*, p. 157-161.

[28] G. Redondo, *Historia de la Iglesia en España*, Madrid, 1993, Vol. I, p. 266.

[29] O. Alzaga Villaamil, La primera democracia cristiana en España, Barcelona, 1973.

he wrote in 1932, "The Work of God was not thought up by a man to remedy the lamentable situation of the Church in Spain since 1931 ... Nor have we come to meet the special needs of a particular time or country, because from the very beginning Jesus has wanted his Work to have a universal heart."[30]

Escriva saw the aim of Opus Dei as promoting among Catholics of all walks of life an awareness of the fact that their baptismal vocation involves a call to personal sanctity and a desire to live out that truth in their daily lives. A sincere personal commitment to striving to model their lives on Christ's life would, Escriva foresaw, lead the members of Opus Dei, and others who lived its spirit, to try to make their society more just and harmonious, more in keeping with Christ's teaching. Their active Christian presence in society would, thus, contribute to making it more Christian. This would not be the result, however, of an effort by Opus Dei to organize Catholics for political activity. Rather it would spring from the personal commitment of its individual members to putting Christ's teachings into practice in their personal lives and in their daily work and other activities, including their political activities.[31] The idea is captured in a point of *The Way:* "A secret. An open secret: these world crises are crises of saints. —God wants a handful of men 'of his own' in every human activity. Then ... 'pax Chrsti in regno Christi'— the peace of Christ in the kingdom of Christ."[32]

The fact that its aim was broader and more comprehensive than politics was not the only difference between Opus Dei and those organizations whose aim was to mobilize Catholics for political action. Such groups were often based on the supposition that all Catholics do and should agree on how best to organize society. Escriva understood that although Catholics should agree on certain basic moral and religious values —such as the dignity of the human person, the sanctity of marriage, and the equality of all men and women before God— they may legitimately differ on how to implement them here and now. In a letter to members of Opus Dei dated January 9, 1932, Escriva urged them to avoid "the desire, contrary to man's licit independence, to force everyone to form a single group in things that are matters of opinion, converting temporal doctrines into dogmas..."[33]

Escriva expected the members of Opus Dei to be guided in their political opinions and activities by Christ's teachings articulated by the Church,[34] but he respected their personal freedom in deciding how those teachings should be

---

[30] Josemaria Escriva, *Instrucción acerca del espiritu sobrenatural de la Obra de Dios*, n. 8 and 15.

[31] J.L. Illanes, "Faith and Personal Freedom in Social and Political Conduct. Thoughts on some teachings of Blessed Josemaría Escriva," *Romana* 31 (2000) pp. 300-324.

[32] *The Way,* n. 301.

[33] *Letter of January 9, 1932,* n. 1.

[34] "Nonsectarianism. Neutrality. Those old myths that always try to seem new. —Have you ever bothered to think how absurd it is to leave one's Catholicism aside on entering a university, or a professional association, or a scholarly meeting, or Congress, as if you were checking your hat at the door?" *The Way,* n. 61.

implemented in the concrete reality of the here and now.[35]

Escriva adhered faithfully to this spirit even in the very difficult early years of the Republic. At a time when the Church was under attack and political passions were running extremely high, it would have been very easy to think that —whatever the value of personal political freedom and autonomy under normal circumstances— the time had come for all believers to join together in a single political front. Short of that, the circumstances would have seemed to justify Escriva's making an effort to point out to his followers specific politically effective ways of implementing Christian principles in the circumstances of the moment. In fact, however, however, Escriva did nothing of the sort.

Quite the contrary. The advice Escriva gave his followers during the difficult early months of the Republic was so spiritual in its focus and so far removed from urging them to take a particular course of political action that it might have been misinterpreted as suggesting disengagement from social and political life.

Shortly after the proclamation of the Republic, for instance, he wrote to Isidoro Zorzano: "Don't worry one way or the other about the political change. Be concerned only that they do not offend God."[36] A few months later, in August, 1931, he wrote to him: "I suppose that all these attacks on our Christ will have served to inflame you even more in his service. Try to belong to him more each day..., with prayer. Offer him also each day, as expiation that is very pleasing in his divine eyes, the annoyances that life continually brings with it."[37]

Standing alone, these texts might seem to suggest indifference to politics and concern only with religious matters. That was not the case. Escriva encouraged an active interest in politics and seriousness in the fulfillment of

---

[35] Escriva often spoke and wrote about the diversity of political opinions among the members of Opus Dei as a sign of good spirit and of a healthy respect for the freedom of others. People who approach the question from a less theological perspective than Escriva may sometimes find it hard to reconcile his statements about the complete freedom of Opus Dei members to adopt any political position with the conspicuous absence of support from Opus Dei members for some positions that are championed by important political groups and parties. The solution to this apparent contradiction lies in the distinction Escriva drew between "political" questions on which Catholics may freely form their own individual opinions (for example, whether there should be a legal minimum wage and if so how much) and the moral and doctrinal teachings of the Church (for example, that workers are entitled to a living wage, and that employers have a moral obligation to pay just wages). He did not consider those moral and doctrinal teachings "political," even though as a sociological matter they might be hotly debated by political parties. If in a particular country one or more political groups supported the position that whatever wages are set by market forces are always just and that the government should never intervene in any way in labor markets, Opus Dei members would not join them in those positions. Their refusal to do so would be a result, however, not of their condition as members of Opus Dei but rather of the fact that they strive to be faithful to the social doctrine of the Church. Escriva would classify their decision not as political but as religious, moral or ethical.

[36] J.M. Pero-Sanz, *Isidoro Zorzano*, Madrid 1996, p. 126.

[37] *Idem*, p. 128

civic responsibilities. In sharp contrast to the clerical one-party mentality that prevailed among Catholics at the time, however, he believed that it was up to individual Catholics to make their own choices about how to implement the Church's teaching in practice. Even in the intensely politicized atmosphere of the early years of the Second Republic, he scrupulously refrained from expressing his own political preferences, limiting himself to encouraging all those who sought his advice to take seriously their civic duties and to exercise their rights as citizens in ways that would make the society more Christian.

Conclusion

On the personal level, the anticlericalism of the early Second Republic offered Escriva many opportunities to grow in self control in the face of insults and attacks directed at him precisely because he was a priest. On the institutional level, it presented an occasion to affirm Opus Dei's determination to remain above the political fray and to concentrate on the spiritual and religious formation of its members and those involved in its apostolic activities, respecting the personal freedom of each of them to form his own political opinions and to act in consequence.

CARLOS CAVALLÉ

TRANSFORMING BUSINESS AND THE COMMON GOOD

Introduction

Business firms are undergoing spectacular changes. The development of new knowledge and the impact of new technologies, along with the globalization of

St. Josemaria at Jaltepec, Guadalajara, Mexico, June 14, 1970.

markets and of the economy, are among the leading factors of these changes. The recent accelerated growth of wealth and well-being, especially in the western world, should be attributed to the efficient and increasingly productive performance of well-organized business. However, society in general is not entirely pleased with some of the results of these changes. Scandals lately reported in the media have prompted strong reactions against malpractice in business, and the business firm itself is under suspicion. Reactions from governments usually take the form of new regulations designed to make it more difficult for business to deceive the market. And within the corporation, new voices speak loudly about the need to reconsider corporate governance. There is the feeling that the current conception of the business firm is not contributing to the common good at the expected and needed level.

New concepts of the business firm are being researched and considered by different parties with the aim of changing the current status quo. But, as modern economic theory recognizes, no changes will take place unless an appropriate set of motivations and incentives are in place. This paper will try to show

how, for many people, the message of St. Josemaria Escriva on the sanctification of ordinary life constitutes a real set of motivations for the transformation of businesses in particular and of work structures in general, to make them better contributors to the common good. By means of a number of examples of professionals who have tried to put such a message into practice, this paper will attempt to prove that transformation is possible, and therefore that there are reasons for hope.

A Humanist Approach to the Business Firm and a Definition of the Common Good

The following three conceptions of the business firm are endorsed by current research and current business practice although, admittedly, to a lesser degree than is desirable. They are also consistent with the teachings of St. Josemaria Escriva.

1. The business firm is increasingly understood as a community of people who, in an organized fashion, pursue the fulfillment of established common objectives that are also compatible with their own legitimate personal objectives.

2. Business firms are also considered to be organizations that can help in the creation and distribution of wealth by providing a quality service, contributing either directly or indirectly to resolving problems of human and social development at an ever-increasing rate. The most developed countries are not those that have more natural resources but rather those that have the best organized businesses.

3. With all of the inherent defects that will need to be corrected over time, the business firm is also considered to be a place for acquiring new knowledge, exercising capabilities, and developing attitudes that contribute (or should contribute) to personal improvement as well as to social progress.

As we will see, these three conceptions are conducive to practicing the teachings of St. Josemaria Escriva in business firms, and can have a positive impact on people in particular and society in general. They can also help us to arrive at a new understanding of what constitutes the common good. The idea of the common good is not insignificant. For a simple definition we can refer to the Second Vatican Council. In point 26 of the constitution *Gaudium et Spes*, the common good is described as "the set of conditions in social life that make it possible for associations and for each one of their members to better achieve their own perfection."

Gaudium et Spes goes on to explain that, given the fact that socio-economic interdependency is ever greater and more universal, the common good is also increasingly universal. This implies rights and obligations in regard to all of mankind. In other words, the common good is becoming an increasingly universal question, and its causes and effects are understood to be increasingly interconnected. Therefore, the positive contributions made through any activity, in any place and by any one person, noticeably affect the general common good, no matter how small these contributions may seem.

This paper tries to show how the message of St. Josemaria, which is received and put into practice in diverse ways and with responsible initiatives by people all over the world, *can* and *does* help the progress and advancement of the common good through professional activities within businesses. I would like to point out that, despite the simple formulation of the common good, the effort to contribute to it is neither an easy nor a trivial task. Quite often, in fact, the process is accompanied by difficulties and frustrations. But the stories of those who have succeeded in this pursuit are proof that it is worth the effort to try.

St. Josemaria on Work and Sanctity

The part of St. Josemaria's message that can be most directly applied to the topic in question is his invitation to men and women of good will to "place Christ, by means of their work in the middle of the world, at the summit of all human activities." And in *Friends of God,* St. Josemaria calls on Christians to attain sanctity in the midst of their daily work:

> It is we, men walking in the street, ordinary Christians immersed in the bloodstream of society, whom Our Lord wants to be Saints and apostles, in the very midst of our professional work; that is, sanctifying our job in life, sanctifying ourselves in it and, through it, helping others to sanctify themselves as well. Be convinced that it is there that God awaits you, with all the love of a Father and Friend.
>
> Consider too that, by doing your daily work well and responsibly, not only will you be supporting yourselves financially but you will also be contributing in a very direct way to the development of society, relieving the burdens of others and maintaining countless welfare projects, both local and international, on behalf of less privileged individuals and countries.[1]

The message of St. Josemaria, expressed in this way, leads to what I call the "two transformations." The first is a personal transformation, whose roots lie in the compact, or covenant, with God the Father and Friend, and whose objective is a union with God by means of ordinary activity. The second is a transformation of the conditions of the working world. The objective of this transformation is to ensure that conditions in the workplace are in the spirit of the teachings of Jesus Christ, in order that they may facilitate and promote reconciliation with God for all of humanity.

III. Personal Testimonies from Around the World

Several years ago, we issued a call for personal accounts of how Josemaria Escriva's message transformed peoples' lives along the lines of the "two transformations" just mentioned. In order to better explain what we were after, we

---

[1] *Friends of God*, 120.

used the parable of the Good Samaritan in the Gospel of St. Luke as an example. It is one of the best-known passages of the New Testament, showing how the generous behavior of one person (the Good Samaritan) transformed the very sad situation of a traveler who had been robbed and badly beaten, by coming to his aid.

The response to our call was also generous and abundant. And at this point we would like to reiterate our thanks to all who contributed their stories. Thanks to their generous response, we have more than 120 personal testimonies from professionals from more than 20 countries. Almost all of these personal accounts have been compiled in an interactive CD-Rom that offers rapid consultation and the possibility of further study.

An initial analysis of the testimonies (which should and surely will be analyzed in greater depth in the future) allows us to put forward some conclusions about how the message of St. Josemaria influenced the respondents as they faced key decision in their lives, and reveals an interesting confluence of professional and Christian meaning.

The testimonies originate from a wide array of professional responsibilities ranging from a California movie director to an owner of a gasoline station in Australia; from a pastry shop owner in Northern Spain to a vice-consul of the United States Embassy; from a television director in France to an automobile parts mogul in Germany.

In general, the personal accounts describe situations in the respondents' professional lives in which the teachings of St. Josemaria invited them to explore a new approach, a change, both in their personal lives and in their professional activities. Thus we can see how a Catalan textile entrepreneur, plagued by a grave crisis in his economic sector, decides not to close or sell his factories because of his desire for justice for his employees. Or how a construction giant eliminates longstanding practices that are considered habitual in the industry and can be described as corrupt, thereby clearly improving the working environment, and elevating the technical level of his company in the process. In other cases, we can see how labor rules are improved in organizations (for example in Kenya) to facilitate the professional careers of women by adopting favorable maternity leave measures that surpass the stipulations of current legislation. Or how ethical criteria are introduced into the processes of contract preparation (in a law firm in Chile), when this is not necessarily the standard practice. But we also find cases that show how to provide for the needs of the less fortunate, helping them to solve housing problems in a Brazilian city or to overcome professional training problems in a Peruvian institute.

The personal accounts found on the CD-Rom are grouped under nine titles in such a way as to facilitate their consultation and study. These titles give an idea of the variety of the personal accounts received:

1. Woman, work, and the common good: The important role that women can and do play in the working world can be made more compatible with their family responsibilities.

2. Attention to the less fortunate: Charity has primacy over justice in business management.

3. Confronting corruption: A Christian approach to life is incompatible with practices that can be qualified as corrupt.

4. Professional competency and the common good: Carrying out professional activities responsibly requires thorough and rigorous professional preparation.

5. Values and virtues in the workplace: The workplace presents a constant opportunity to practice all of the Christian virtues in a charitable way.

6. Work ethic: Ethical principles facilitate the overall development of individuals.

7. Personal and professional responsibilities: Equilibrium among one's family, one's profession, and one's relationship with God is needed in order to lead a coherent Christian life. This equilibrium is also feasible.

8. Social dimension of the businessperson: By assuming business risks one can help others by creating jobs and facilitating training opportunities.

9. Forging a more human enterprise: Human beings, created in the image and likeness of God, have dignity and rights that should be respected.

Upon analyzing these personal accounts, we see that they have points in common. We note in a positive vein that in all cases the message of St. Josemaria has helped people to improve at work and to improve work itself. However, we also note the emergence of a pattern of behavioral principles throughout the personal accounts that are worthy of in-depth study. In the following pages, I will attempt to describe the behavioral principles that are common to the various personal testimonies. Although much of this will be familiar to those who are acquainted with and have sought to put into practice the teachings of St. Josemaria, the personal accounts carry added weight in view of the fact that they describe real situations. Moreover the impact is heightened because the testimonies reveal the effort people put into transforming themselves and their workplaces in the hope and with the goal of more closely following our Lord, and thus better serving society in general and people in particular.

Personal Transformation through Professional Work[2]

Although the personal transformations that can be seen in the testimonies follow different paths, they have in common points that St. Josemaria expresses with great clarity about the sanctification of ordinary life and the sanctification of one's work. We will highlight four such points by providing brief quotes from the personal accounts received, and passages from St. Josemaria.

---

[2] The personal accounts included in the text of this paper are excerpts from the complete accounts contained in the CD-Rom prepared for the occasion of the Centennial of the Blessed Josemaria Escrivà.

1. Professional work done with professional competence and with an attitude of service is a necessary condition for personal improvement and union with God.

For 23 years I have been working in the Workplace Accident Insurance Division of the Mutual de Seguridad in Chile, a company that currently employs 2300 workers.

When I discovered the message of St. Josemaria it made clear the meaning of my Christian vocation, the dignity of "being a son of God," and the calling to sanctify myself in my work. All of this changed my way of approaching my professional life.

Our "managers' table" was a jumble of diverse and conflicting currents of philosophical, political, and religious thinking that made the topics of conversation at our lunch hour a constant challenge for me. But the most significant part of it was that the ethical dimension of business decisions was not always taken into account. And this was an issue that I had to do something about.

In addition to emphasize respect for the law, I tried to introduce a "business ideology" based on respect for others and the importance, in all fields, of justice as well as ethical and human factors, in accordance with the Social Doctrine of the Church.

At the outset, my colleagues—in keeping with a Chilean custom—branded me a "road block" to the development of business due to my legal background and my emphasis on ethics.

As time went by, they realized in the company that my observations, always made in writing, maintained coherence between what is legal and what is ethical, between what is legal and what is fair, between what is legal and what is honest in business, between what is legal and the firmness of principles and values. I also managed to support these reports with oral presentations, conversing individually or collectively with the interested parties in order to give them a Christian focus on the matters at hand.

The managers began to notice that the former "road block" had become a friend who, over time, facilitated dialogue and the rapid processing of activities. For this reason, they convinced the executives and professionals from other contracting parties to request my presence in negotiations. In this way, it became natural to study the ethical dimensions of the decisions in our company. As we did it, it became part of the reputation of our company.

"Professional work, whatever it is, becomes a lamp to enlighten your colleagues and friends. That is why I usually tell those who become members of

The reference for the CD-Rom is as follows:
The grandeur of ordinary life
International Congress
Rome, January 8 – 11, 2002
Work session: **Business and the Common Good**
Text selection elaborated by *Prof. Carlos Cavallé*, IESE Business School. University of Navarra
IESE Publishing
Avda. Pearson, 21
08034 Barcelona

Opus Dei, and the same applies to all of you now listening to me: 'What use is it telling me that so and so is a good son of mine — a good Christian — but a bad shoemaker?' If he doesn't try to learn his trade well, or doesn't give his full attention to it, he won't be able to sanctify it or offer it to Our Lord. The sanctification of ordinary work is, as it were, the hinge of true spirituality for people who, like us, have decided to come close to God while being at the same time fully involved in temporal affairs." [3]

2. Perfection and attention to details in one's work, no matter how humble or insignificant it may seem, create the conditions for personal transformation.

Mathew runs a human resources company in Kenya. His attitude toward service allows him to place emphasis on small details, as St. Josemaria constantly preached. These small details include, among other things, not making people who come to his office wait unnecessarily. To do this, he set up a registry for the arrival time and the time he begins attending to each person, reviewing it periodically and thus helping improve his own service.

"What I have always taught over the last forty years is that a Christian should do all honest human work, be it intellectual or manual, with the greatest perfection possible: with human perfection (professional competence) and with Christian perfection (for love of God's Will and as a service to mankind). Human work done in this manner, no matter how humble or insignificant it may seem, helps to shape the world in a Christian way." (Conversations, 10)

3. Christians should realize the importance of solidarity (charity) above and beyond justice in the execution of professional responsibilities.

I am an entrepreneur and supplier of automotive parts in Germany. In the mid-90's, the price of raw materials began to undergo spectacular hikes, and many companies in our sector had serious problems. As a result, the production of automobiles dropped in all of Europe. Parts buyers pressured suppliers by imposing low prices via methods that, until then, were unheard of. During this period, many small and medium companies threw in the towel. The best sold themselves to large conglomerates, almost all of which were capitalized with U.S. money.

My company, like my competitors, was the object of a number of exploratory contacts and promising offers. At that time, this represented a gleam of hope, a relief for owners and managers, and also the temptation to follow the easiest path, which was surely not the best path for our employees. It was legal, it was accepted by the unions, but it was not what I felt I should do.

Moved by the duty of solidarity and charity, which is clearly expressed in the teachings of John Paul II and St. Josemaria, I decided not to sell the family business. I explained my reasons to the other members of the family and to my employees and, together with them, set a demanding cost-cutting and inno-

---

[3]*Friends of God*, 61. 08034 Barcelona

vation plan in motion. With the help of God, we began surmounting the crisis little by little.

Today, our business has grown in volume and in quality; we have increased our staff, we offer new and better products, and we have excellent long-term projects that are already under development.

"Charity perfects and completes justice. It moves us to respond differently to different people, adapting ourselves to their specific circumstances ... Justice says that each person should receive his due, which does not mean giving the same to everyone. Utopian egalitarianism can give rise to the greatest injustice."[4]

4. Charity facilitates the development of all other virtues, which are increasingly demanded in the fulfillment of the responsibilities of any business professional.

I am a vice consul of my country, and every day I have to deal with the numerous—at times enormous—personal problems of my compatriots. While I listen to them or read their letters, I cannot remain indifferent: I pray for them, as I learned from St. Josemaria, and I often succeed —in addition to attempting to solve their problems— in offering them a supernatural perspective.

The other day, I had to deal with the case of a young man facing criminal charges. I visited him, I promised myself that he would receive legal assistance and I helped, to the extent possible, with his poor family. I listened to them and took charge of their situation. They, in turn, began adopting a different attitude when they saw that they were understood and respected, to the point where the accused himself began to change, accepting his punishment as something deserved, and deciding to serve his time in prison and become another Christ, as St. Josemaria emphasized, thinking about the thousand different circumstances we humans can go through.

"By living charity—Love—you live all the human and supernatural virtues demanded of a Christian. These virtues form a unity and cannot be reduced to a mere list. You cannot have charity without justice, solidarity, family and social responsibility, poverty, joy, friendship..."[5]

Transforming the Structures and Conditions of Work

If we focus now on what the personal accounts say about the sanctification of work, it is clear that the transformation of work structures is not a trivial effort. It usually constitutes a life-long project for a business professional. The variety of human circumstances, cultures, and economic and social developments only adds complexity to the search for better, more human, more Christian solutions. Despite this complexity, the personal accounts clearly lay out certain behavioral principles that ought to preside over any effort to transform the

---

[4] *Friends of God, 173*

[5] *Conversations with Mgr. Escriva de Balaguer, 62.*

structure of work. These principles are part of the message of St. Josemaria. The majority of personal accounts relate to these principles. I have selected seven, which I should now like to cite.

1. The first duty in transforming work structures is the recognition of the dignity of the individual and thus of any work that an individual carries out.

I am an electrical engineer and have been working for electric companies for almost thirty years now. Since January of 2001, I have been responsible for a new company that provides high-tension electrical transmission service to most of Wisconsin along with various zones in its neighboring states of Michigan and Illinois.

In retrospect, I have contemplated the extent to which the teachings of St. Josemaria have influenced my professional work in two important ways: in my attitude towards work itself and in my relationships with others, i.e. employees, colleagues, suppliers and even competitors.

St. Josemaria underscored the need for continuous study as a necessary base for an efficient professional work effort. Not long ago, an old partner of mine was asking me if I still studied on a daily basis. We had debated this topic when we began our careers, and the truth is that I have maintained this practice right up to now. By doing so, I have received two university degrees, along with the conviction of the necessity to promote and run training programs for mechanics and electricians as well as professional employees in my division. These programs have been crucial, as many of these employees have updated their knowledge, progressed in their careers, and improved their salaries.

Over the years, I have had the occasion to manage the work of employees across all levels and with various union representatives. Convinced of the dignity of all honest work and the respect that all individuals deserve regardless of their class or category, I have succeeded in establishing and maintaining excellent relationships with all of my employees and their union representatives. To do this, it was necessary to break down implicit class barriers between employees with union representation and employees with supervisory roles. I made consulting the employees about all matters affecting their work a habitual practice, and it was clear how much they appreciated it when their knowledge and experience was recognized.

"It is time for us Christians to shout from the rooftops that work is a gift from God and that it makes no sense to classify men differently, according to their occupation, as if some jobs were nobler than others. Work, all work, bears witness to the dignity of man, to his dominion over creation. It is an opportunity to develop one's personality. It is a bond of union with others, the way to support one's family, a means of aiding in the improvement of the society in which we live and in the progress of all humanity."[6]

---

[6] *Christ Is Passing By,* 47

2. It is very important that business be transformed in such a way as to offer dignified jobs and the corresponding education to all employees; these are basic rights for every individual.

Fritz is an entrepreneur from the Philippines who works in the agricultural sector. There he saw firsthand the low professional capacity demanded of workers. He witnessed how the children of farmers abandoned the countryside and fled to the cities without preparation or possibilities. Moved by his sense of social responsibility, enhanced by the teachings of St. Josemaria, he started Agrarian Family Schools in order to prepare farmers professionally and to provide more dignified jobs in the cities for those who wanted to leave their farms.

3. The social principles that derive from Christian thinking, a heritage of western civilization, should be applied in the design and execution of work.

Rosa, a pastry chef and grandmother from Pamplona, touches on this in her story: Although I studied journalism, I have been running this family business, Pastelerías Manterola, for many years now. When the Association of Women Entrepreneurs and Managers awarded me their 1st annual Prize for Navarra's outstanding female entrepreneur, I was overcome. It was a stimulus to continue working for the remainder of my career. The awarding of this prize has made me relive the tragic circumstances under which I took charge of the family business: first, a boat accident that took the lives of my two sisters and my two brothers-in-law, leaving six small children orphaned; then, the death of my husband and one of my daughters in a highway accident.

In this situation, I had to move forward with my eight children and take charge of the business that my husband had run up until then. When I came across the message of St. Josemaria as a young person, it provided me with the supernatural vision necessary to confront reality, as well as the strength not to fall into heartbreak and despair. How does one go forward without prayer?

The years following the accident were truly hard, above all because of the absence of my husband and my daughter. In addition, I had to give strength to the rest of the family. But thanks to God and St. Josemaria, my life and my family have progressed with hard work and effort, while never losing our sense of happiness. I accepted my new job with great professionalism, visiting foreign businesses that were similar to mine and learning from others how to manage and resolve practical issues that were presented to me. Things went well, and I succeeded in expanding the business.

In the means of formation of Opus Dei, it was recommended that I read the documents of the Church on the work of entrepreneurs. One of the documents that helped me most was the encyclical of John Paul II titled "Laborem Exercens," from which I extracted many ideas. One of the Pope's statements had a particularly strong impact on me: "At this time, creating jobs is the best social work that can be done." I understood that this was the path that God had chosen for me — to maintain the job positions in my company and, if possible, create new ones.

4. Work structures become dignified when they facilitate the attitude of service, stimulate the perfection of personal capacities, and lead to the necessary level of professional competence.

I got to know the message of St. Josemaria when I was fifteen. Later on, while I was studying at the University of São Paulo in the late 70's, I began to better understand the spirit of Opus Dei that has since marked my life.

After graduating with a degree in civil engineering, I returned to my city, Ribeirão Preto, and immediately created a construction company that I called Servisa in order to bear in mind at all times that we are here to serve and that it is in our jobs that we must sanctify ourselves by doing efficient work, paying dignified salaries, and offering quality products at fair prices and financed directly at interest rates that are adjusted to people's possibilities.

In fact, in Brazil it was common practice to employ a financing system that made it impossible in the long run to pay off a debt. This was a system that banks and construction companies took advantage of.

It was clear to me that I was not going to get rich by taking the path I had chosen, but this did not really bother me. Currently, I have already constructed apartments for four hundred families, I have provided work for many people and I have made my family successful.

My wife, who is an architect, has been the greatest help in my business. She is the one who plans the apartments and common spaces for the buildings so that family life can run smoothly and well. At the same time, she succeeds in dedicating an important percentage of the land to creating open spaces in which children can play and people can coexist.

Inspired by the teachings of St. Josemaria, both of us have furthermore endeavored to make our life's work compatible with dedication to family.

"The 'miracle' which God asks of you is to persevere in your Christian and divine vocation, sanctifying each day's work: the miracle of turning the prose of each day into heroic verse by the love which you put into your ordinary work. God waits for you there. He expects you to be a responsible person, with the zeal of an apostle and the competence of a good worker.

And so, as the motto of your work, I can give you this one: If you want to be useful, serve. For, in the first place, in order to do things properly, you must know how to do them. I cannot see the integrity of a person who does not strive to attain professional skills and to carry out properly the task entrusted to his care. It's not enough to want to do good; we must know how to do it. And, if our desire is real, it will show itself in the effort we make to use the right methods, finishing things well, achieving human perfection."[7]

5. The personal accounts confirm that business activity should not be limited to the simple reaping of profits or the survival of the business. Instead it

[7] *Christ is Passing By, 50.*

should seek to expand responsibilities in search of the common good. This is not limited to the best distribution of added value. This demands the transformation of circumstances that allow and facilitate the complete development of all individuals that make up the organization or are related to it.

My name is Serah Mwangi. I joined the publishing sector in 1991 when, along with my sister Rose and two friends, I established Focus Publications Ltd., of which I am general manager. We founded Focus Publications Ltd. with the hope of responding to one of St. Josemaria's great desires: to fill the world with "books of fire" in service of the truth.

Many of the authors that come to us have very little experience. When we discover potentially good writers, we spare no effort to help them fully develop their talents. We succeed in keeping our relationship alive with them in order to inculcate the habit of transmitting noble human values in their writing. This demands having long conversations with our authors, filling them with an optimistic and positive outlook on life, even when the tone of the arguments in their books is gray. Often times, it is an arduous task to make authors see that their books will sell without needing to resort to morbid interest. We have experienced great joys in this field: three novels published by us have won national and international awards, in addition to selling well.

Another front on which we must fight involves our printers. Offering quality books requires lots of time and patience. Some printers have a hard time understanding why we care so much about ensuring an equal registry in all the pages of a book or the same ink intensity or a good cut on the edges of the paper so that the spine of the book does not break. When we insist that they pay attention to these "minor" details, they categorize us as difficult clients. Nevertheless, little by little, it is possible to see certain improvements in the finished quality of the books, and even the printers themselves end up taking pride in the quality of their work.

6. The business firm should stay ahead of the knowledge and skills requirements of its employees, provide the proper training, and thus provide a greater level of employability.

I am a co-owner of DieselPro, a small Philippines-based business dedicated to the service and maintenance of diesel injection motors and the sale of component parts for these kinds of machines.

The company was about to shut down during the Asian financial crisis of 1997, the year in which debts doubled due to the change in currency values: our components were all imported. The teachings of St. Josemaria helped me in a decisive way to overcome the critical situation.

Today, after three years of tiring work, the company's debt is 80% paid and has ceased to be a major concern. Through honorable service and efficient work —guidelines that I succeeded in inculcating in my employees— our clientele has quadrupled since 1997.

Today, DieselPro is recognized as one of the country's best companies specializing in the calibration of diesel injection tanks and injectors. For the most part, my employees come from the provinces and are people who have received little or no formal education. But now they are recognized as experienced technicians in the diesel motor sector.

They are motivated to work well, a quality for which they receive recognition not only in their pay but also in a percentage on every job they complete. In 1993, they earned the minimum wage. Presently they earn three times that rate. One of the technicians who has been with the company for a long time wants to retire early and open a tricycle business in his home town of Marinduque. Another has begun to build himself a house in Ilocos, where he will be able to live permanently with his family. My personal goal is to have the workers become co-owners of the company in the near future.

7. The transformation of work structures entails the fostering of an environment conducive to the practice and development of Christian virtues, including respect for and fulfillment of the law, acting against corrupt behavior and encouraging ethical behavior of the part of all employees.

For many years I have been working as the manager of a gasoline station that belongs to an important chain in the sector. One day I met George, who was a member of Opus Dei. We became good friends, and with time I began to attend the means of formation that were being offered at a center of the Work, and began to understand and try to put to practice the message of St. Josemaria Escriva.

After some time had passed, George visited me at work. When he entered the gas station, he looked at the newspaper and magazine kiosk (it was hard not to notice since it occupied a prominent position in the station). On the shelves there were a good number of pornographic magazines. That time George did not say anything, but he prepared his arguments and spoke to me the next time he came by the station.

How could George suggest that I remove the most profitable magazines from my kiosk?

I adopted a defensive attitude, explaining that these magazines were the items that provided the highest margin for the store and that, from a commercial viewpoint, it would be crazy to remove them. George, however, would not back down easily and approached the topic with different lines of argumentation. From my standpoint, I admit that I was not feeling very much at ease. The words of Jesus concerning those who scandalize the young weighed heavily on me, and. And so, from that moment on, I promised George to study the matter seriously. His attitude helped me to understand something that I had heard in many conversations without thinking that it could affect me.

When George next came back to the gas station, he received a pleasant surprise. The magazines were gone, and I had decided to give a new focus to the business, orienting it toward the good of families. I knew that God would not abandon me.

Content with my decision, I tried to convince my colleagues to do the same and stop selling this type of material in their service stations. I spoke with those with whom I had the greatest confidence. This effort turned out to be much more arduous than remodeling my own business, and the reactions I received were by no means favorable: "Since when do you mix your religion with business?" they asked me. Bewildered,

I used commercial arguments – there were more honorable families than depraved truck drivers, as well as Christian arguments – it is illicit to cooperate with evil. After a long discussion, they went their separate ways, disagreeing with everything that I had said to them.

I did not abandon them. In fact, I prayed for them and entrusted them to St. Josemaria. A few days later, I received a phone call. One of my friends was calling to tell me that after our meeting, they had continued discussing the issue and had decided to implement a policy in the other gas stations in favor of families.

"Being a Christian is not something incidental; it is a divine reality that takes root deep in our life. It gives us a clear vision and strengthens our will to act as God wants. So we learn that the Christian's pilgrimage in the world must express itself in a continuous service in all kinds of ways, varying with each person's circumstances, but always motivated by love of God and of our neighbour."[8]

VI. Conclusion

The practical experiences offered in this paper, which are inspired by the original message of St. Josemaria concerning the sanctification of ordinary work, express the power and potential of his message when it is put into practice by professional men and women. The study of these experiences will plant the seeds for new and interesting reflections and open new lines of future thought to benefit businesses and their contribution to the common good.

---

[8] *Christ is Passing By*, 98.

JENNY DRIVER

FROM TOXICITY TO TRANSCENDENCE:
ST. JOSEMARIA AND CONTEMPLATION IN THE WORKPLACE

I am a physician, not an expert in theology or philosophy, and I never knew St. Josemaria personally. I do, however, consider myself an expert in one thing: stress. Like many of my colleagues, I am a connoisseur of stress. We have an ice-cream shop in the United States called Baskin-Robbins. It has forty-one flavors, and if stress came in forty-one flavors, I would have tasted each and every one of them. A recent poll listed medical internship as one of the top five most stressful jobs in the US.

On July 1, the first day of internship, the only people in teaching hospitals more nervous than the new interns are the patients who know that they are being cared for by green recruits, fresh out of medical school. My first night on call, I was awakened by a page from an anxious-sounding nurse who said, "Come quick. Mr. Jones's heart rate is in the 200's and I can't find his pulse." That was the beginning of a love-hate relationship with my pager. On busy days my pager would go off 40 to 50 times, calling me to emergencies or asking for sleeping pills or enemas. Occasionally we would receive a welcome message from a friend, like "let's eat." We called that "friendly fire." Eating, sleeping and other functions we had once considered vital became subject to the dictates of our pagers and the condition of our patients. During my internship year it was routine to work 30-hour shifts and 120-hour workweeks in the intensive care unit, caring for the city's sickest patients on a few hours of sleep, or none. We worked with little to no sleep, fueled by caffeine, adrenaline and the fear of making a mistake.

Within a few months of internship, the idealism with which we initially embraced our job gave way to a kind of cynicism. This is reflected in the slang commonly used in the hospital subculture. Patients who were very sick and not likely to leave the hospital soon became "rocks." One might ask an intern on the geriatrics service. How big is your rock garden?" Getting a new patient from the emergency room during a night on call was called "taking a hit." We began to use "torture" analogies to describe our work. "I really got flogged with pages last night..." Or, "I was hit hard."

We helped each other work through experiences like having to tell a young mother that she was full of cancer, or making an error that led to a patient's death. The emotional, physical and existential stress took its toll on us. The changes in personality produced by this stress were described as "becoming toxic." It was an accepted part of the job, and we learned to overlook our colleagues' depression and irritability as "toxicity." Each one of us ultimately faced the questions, "Why am I doing this? What is the meaning of my patient's suffering? What is the value of my work?"

But there was no time to think about or answer these questions. Products of a contemplatively challenged society with few spiritual roots, the majority of us kept working and kept going, hoping that the angst brought on by our work would pass with time. My workplace was desperately in need of a soul. That need was met by St. Josemaria's teaching about the possibility of contemplation in the midst of a frenetic work life, which helped me to transform my work from an experience of sheer stress into a place where I can encounter God.

My experience of contemplation and an inner life began on a Himalayan peak in Northern India, surrounded by Tibetan prayer flags, thin bits of cloth whipping in the wind, as if echoing the prayers of pilgrims before me who had climbed the mountain in search of peace and spiritual help. I added my brightly colored flags to the faded and tattered ones. I had left my home, my culture and my religion behind and was spending my junior year abroad in India. A poster child for generation X, I had been baptized Catholic but fell away from the Church in childhood despite the example of a very devout mother and a Catholic education. I was turned off by what I considered to be the "corruption of organized religion" and the materialism of my society.

When I went off to college I had a deep spiritual longing. I majored in –isms and Indian Studies and longed to "escape" from the world and from the ordinary. In Existentialism 101 I was intrigued by Martin Heidegger's concept of "authentic existence," a state of "mindfulness of being" in contrast to the "forgetfulness of being" in which one surrenders to the everyday world and becomes lost in its concerns. I lived a double life—my spiritual interests were my own, private quest and were not integrated with the reality of my social and school life.

I climbed the mountain because there, far away from the worries and stresses of the world, I felt peaceful. I was able to forget about the contradictions and inconsistencies of my own life. It was easy to have a spirituality that demanded nothing of me that I didn't want to give. I felt I had escaped the "world" and material things with all their negative influence on me. I had moments of light and inspiration. Once, when I was spending time in Darmsella, in Northern India, where the Dalai Lama lived in exile, I noticed that bells would ring at odd times. I wondered what they meant. I went up to an elderly Tibetan woman, and asked her what the bells were for. She smiled and laughed: "They are to remind you that it is now." At that time, I did not grasp the meaning of her words. It was only later, much later, through the words of St. Josemaria, that I came to understand them.

As soon as I returned from India, my Buddhist veneer wore off. Fighting with my brothers and full of complaints, I was really longing for my mountain. I had no way of integrating my "spirituality" with the reality of each day.

It was about that time that my mother introduced me to some women in Opus Dei. I was immediately fascinated by their ideal of being contemplatives in the middle of the world, something I thought to be a contradiction. I was moved by their obvious love for and intimacy with God, who was a person to them, someone loving and understanding. These women were busy professionals, and threw themselves into their work, but somehow had a depth and peace that helped them absorb the bumps in the road that seemed the throw me off kilter. Through my friends in Opus Dei and the life and teaching of St. Josemaria, I came to a deeper understanding of the truths of the Catholic faith. I began to pray and came back to the Sacraments. I no longer needed a mountain–retreat to feel close to God. I had discovered Him in the center of my soul. And even when I was peeling potatoes—I sometimes do!

The quest to live with constant knowledge of God's presence and providence was the "authentic existence" I had been searching for. So much of my life had been spent living on a level of worry and stress, trying to be "in control" and railing against my limitations. Rarely living in or enjoying the present moment, I ruminated on the past or was concerned about the future, having unrealistic expectations like "saving" all of my patients, never making mistakes, or always "looking good" to others. I realize how little I listened to people, how my worries about work and the people I loved crowded my consciousness.

I began to understand the inner struggle that was needed in order to overcome the restlessness and anxiety which had characterized my life to that point, and the transforming power of the sense of being a child of God. God was no longer an impersonal spectator, or harsh critic, but rather a loving person, who was intimately involved in the happenings of each moment. St. Josemaria described this awareness of being a beloved child of God as divine filiation. It is the wellspring from which his whole spiritual life flowed.

So much of my 'toxicity" stemmed from a lack of inner life and not knowing how to have balance in my life or expectations. Martha was toxic when she complained to Jesus that Mary wasn't helping. It wasn't because Martha was working and Mary was loving. It was because Martha didn't see that work could be love. She had forgotten that God himself was so close to her and that through her work she was serving Him. She was thinking only of herself and this is what led to her unhappiness.

As is described beautifully in Dr. Coverdale's book, in a moment of incredible stress, when everything seemed to be going against him, St. Josemaria sat on a streetcar, and was suffused with a deep, profound, and permanent knowledge of, and confidence in, God's love for him. That confidence, that experience, of knowing that he was a beloved child of God, was what allowed him to continue and become the person that we heard about this morning. This was a life-transforming moment for St. Josemaria. It enabled him to have an incredible optimism and resilience in the face of disappointments, disasters, and betrayals of all kinds. His whole life is a testament to the power of one who knows how to become a child.

This power is beautifully illustrated by a vignette I read many years ago. It occurred during the terrible earthquake in Armenia that I'm sure many of you remember. A grade school had been leveled, and large number of children were buried and presumed dead. There was no heavy machinery available to help remove the rubble. Long after the other parents had given up from exhaustion, one man doggedly continued digging for over twenty-four hours, until finally he heard the voice of his child. He was saying, "Daddy, I knew you would come. I knew you would come." He just kept repeating that. It took a number of hours to actually extricate the child completely, and later relief workers marveled at that child's apparent lack of post-traumatic stress disorder, which many people can have after a horrible experience like that. For the child, the experience had only confirmed the love of his father for him. I remembered this story in the days following September 11, as I saw the toll that event had taken on my patients, who have cancer, and on their families. A young child is buried alive, but survives unscathed, while thousands of people are shaken to their core, and require anti-depressants or anti-anxiety medication, because of an event they witnessed on television. At its roots, anxiety is a fear of loss, a fear of rejection, a fear of meaninglessness. It comes from living without a sense of the providence of God, or from losing it.

St. Josemaria often repeated and meditated on the words "Omnia in bonum": All things work together for the good of those who love God. He said, "My children, see God behind every event and circumstance." It has always interested me that the Chinese character for "crisis" is the same as for "opportunity." For St. Josemaria, accepting the events of each day as the will of God gave them a new meaning. Each "crisis" was now an opportunity for union with God and growth in virtue.

He used to say, "Don't say, 'That person bothers me.' Think that person sanctifies me." This simple advice has helped me to see the difficult situations I encounter in my work as something positive, something God sends me so I can grow in some way. This point of view gives my work a sense of meaning. It has even helped me to be on better terms with my beeper. Instead of swearing every time it goes off, I have learned over time to think, "God is calling me."

In Christian terms, as I carry out my work for God, I am somehow participating in his plans to make the world, and myself, better. I begin to see the value of the mundane and the monotonous. I am able to have contemplative moments throughout my day. When I write prescriptions, I picture the face of the patient I am helping. When sit down to do dictations, I offer that hour as a prayer for the patients whose stories I am telling. When I go to visit a dying patient, I take their hand and comfort them in some way and I become Veronica, wiping the face of Christ. As St. Josemaria would say, the ordinary happenings of my working day can "sanctify" me. In other words, I become less centered on myself and more on God and others.

Here is another quote that I love: "I will never share the opinion- though I respect it- of those who separate prayer from active life, as if they were incompatible. We children of God have to be contemplatives: people who, in the midst of the din and the throng, know how to find silence of soul in a lasting conversation with our Lord, people who know how to look at him as they look at a Father, as they look at a Friend, as they look at someone with whom they are madly in love."[1]

---

[1] *Forge,* 738.

I do battle with the things that separate me from God and lead me to anxiety and toxicity on many fronts. E-mail is an ever-present temptation, addiction and vortex. I realized that it had become a source of anxiety for me and led me to interrupt my work and not work well. So I only check it twice a day. What a conquest! The daily struggle to put my work down when it's time to go is another thing I have learned, based on the inspiration of St. Josemaria. In that way my work doesn't dominate me.

There are many beautiful stories of how the Spirit of Opus Dei has helped people to find meaning in their work and do it for the love of God and others. One that has stuck with me particularly is about a friend who is a member of Opus Dei who runs a very large hotel in Houston. As you may know, there is a huge medical center in Houston. People come from all over the world for treatment. My friend gives people who work in her hotel inspirational talks every week about their work, trying to inspire them to do their work well. One day, one of her employees, someone who made up the rooms, cleaned them and changed the sheets, said to her, "I just want to thank you, because ever since one of your talks when you told us about that priest and his work, every time I make a bed I think I'm helping the family of some small child who has leukemia and who is here for treatment. And I love my job now."

There is another story that has always stuck with me. When one works in a contemplative way, one has amazing effects on the people around you. This is a true story. It happened in a prison in mainland China. There was a political prisoner in solitary confinement, and he had only one little window he could look out of to try to connect with the outside world. And every day there was a man who came and swept the courtyard outside of the window. It was the same man every day, and the way that man did his job saved the life of the man in confinement. It saved his sanity. Every day he would look out at the man as he swept. The man didn't do just a cursory job. He swept beautifully; if he missed a spot he went back and got it. And he worked with such a sense of purpose. That little thing allowed the man in solitary confinement to think, "There has to be a meaning in what I am going through, and I can make it to the end." This is a man without any specific faith. After they were both released from the prison, the man who had been in solitary confinement found out that the other man had been a Catholic bishop who had been in prison for, I think, over twenty years. Every day, when he swept, he was offering his work to God.

But Christianity is not an inoculation against the daily struggle with our weaknesses, unexpected contradictions, friction with others, and fatigue. Christ himself faced and embraced the difficulties of being human. I have a lot of devotion to the stressed Jesus, the tired Jesus, the anxious Jesus. Jesus' public life was a lot like internship and residency. He was up all night and had no time to sleep or eat; he went from one patient to the next. Jesus showed his infinite wisdom by choosing to come to earth in the pre-beeper era, but people managed to find him even when he tried to hide. Jesus even got "toxic" to show us his humanity. There is a beautiful scene where he is with the apostles, and they are trying to cure someone, and they are just not making it—they can't cut it.

There is a big scene, and they pull him in and ask, "Why can't we sure this man?" And the first thing Jesus does is to look up to heaven and say, "O faithless and unbelieving generation. How long must I put up with you?" That has given me a lot of consolation, and a lot of devotion to the humanity of Christ, who chose to experience the frustration that we all experience every day.

How did he do it? Christ drew his strength from his rich inner life, nourished by prayer. He saw things with a supernatural vision and was spurred on by his mission, to redeem humanity out of love. He embraced every moment as full of meaning and saw it with the perspective of eternity.

Through my friends in Opus Dei, I discovered the joy and the adventure of developing an inner life. I began to dedicate time to prayer and draw strength from the sacraments. I began to see that my desk is my altar, the place I can sacrifice myself for others, the place I can encounter God. On a good day, I accept the double bookings, emergency calls at 5 p.m. on Friday, patients who arrive an hour late, and hours of disability forms as coming from God's hands; on my bad days, my job is a flog and I can get quite "toxic." Every day I start again.

In addition to bringing me closer to God, my work gives me the opportunity to reach out to others. I try to do this more by my example than my words. As most of my patients have cancer, there are many opportunities to affirm their dignity and speak with them about their spiritual concerns. I'm sure you are familiar with the old adage that there are no atheists in foxholes. Well, I can tell you that there are very few atheists among those who are struggling with cancer. As a devout Catholic in an agnostic academic environment, I try to open the minds of my colleagues to the concept of a loving God and the possibility of an inner life. Through my profession as an oncologist and teacher I try to help foster respect for the elderly and the dying. I sometimes find it hard to swim against the tide and have to ask for more courage.

There is a beautiful quote in an article by Cardinal Ratzinger written around the time of the canonization of St. Josemaria, in which he describes this sense of divine filiation, and the effects that it can have for the individual person and for the world. He says, " Those who have this link with God, those who have this uninterrupted conversation with him, can dare to respond to challenges and are no longer afraid because those who are in God's hands always fall into God's hands. This is how fear disappears and courage is born to respond to the contemporary world."

I'm eternally grateful to St. Josemaria for helping me to realize that I didn't need to go to the top of the mountain in order to find God, and that I could find Him in the center of my soul. I would like to end with these words of his: "My children, heaven and earth seem to merge on the horizon. But where they really meet is in your heart."[2]

---

[2] St. Josemaria Escriva, "Passionately Loving the World," paragraph 16.

CLIFFORD ORWIN

RESPONSE TO THE PAPERS OF JENNY DRIVER AND CARLOS CAVALLÉ, WITH REPLIES BY DRIVER AND CAVALLÉ

I am certainly the odd man out at this panel, being neither a devotee of St. Josemaria, nor a Catholic, nor even a Christian. I view only from the outside the life and example of the remarkable man whom you are able to view as your own. Of course that's why I was invited: I am to provide an outside perspective, and in that respect at least I can't possibly fail.

In fact, in my role of designated outsider I am going to give you double your money's worth. In commenting on these two powerful papers I will adopt perspectives external not just to those of the authors but to my own. In my remarks on Dr. Driver's paper, for instance, you will hear from Orwin the Conventional Liberal (even though the actual Orwin is at most an Unconventional Liberal.) I will play this role for fear that no one else at this gathering will do so, and because I'm eager to hear Dr.. Driver's response to an objection couched in these terms. That may help me learn how to respond to it; Lord knows I've heard it often enough from critics of Opus Dei.

All right, then. As a liberal, I declaim as follows. The nerve of Dr. Driver in introducing Christianity into her medical practice. Doesn't she see that the same liberal tolerance that smiles on her practicing her religion in its proper place frowns on her introducing it into the workplace? For our liberal way of life excludes religion from the public sphere, and the workplace is increasingly (and properly) conceived as pertaining to the public sphere. That's why we must maintain it quite strictly as everything neutral. You know what I mean: race neutral, gender neutral, culture neutral, sexual preference neutral. All right, not smoking neutral, I'll grant you that, but certainly faith neutral. The workplace must be perfectly, indiscriminately inclusive, and so while adherents of all religions are welcome, they must park those religions at the door. This is why we liberals distrust you in Opus Dei; you may call yourselves God's Work, but God's Work has no place in the workplace. Certainly not in Dr. Driver's workplace, dedicated as it is to the Baconian project of the relief of man's estate.

This critique seems to me to pose a greater practical obstacle to Dr. Driver's Christian aspirations than she acknowledges in her statement. She does acknowledge it as a significant one. "As a devout Catholic in an agnostic academic environment, I try to open the minds of my colleagues to the concept of a loving God and the possibility of an inner life. ... I sometimes find it hard to swim against the tide and have to ask for more courage." What Dr. Driver doesn't say is whether working in an agnostic academic environment, she experiences conflict between the demands she places on herself as a Christian and the demands of that environment.

I hope that I won't embarrass Dr. Driver if I compare her situation with that of the venerable religious who will soon join Father Escriva among the saints of the Church, Mother Teresa of Calcutta. I turn to Mother Teresa *faute de mieux,* because I don't know much about recent paragons of Catholicism but I do know something about her. I'm writing a book on the role of compassion in modern society, and I felt that to this end there was nothing more important for me to grasp than the distinction between true Christian charity and this its ersatz modern successor. In the book I adopt Princess Diana as my icon of secular compassion, and Mother Teresa as my model of Christian charity.

One of the writers on Mother Teresa I found most useful for clarifying her greatness was the most virulent of her detractors, the British journalist Christopher Hitchens. Aggressively secular, antireligious in general and anti-Catholic in particular, Hitchens hated Mother Teresa for the best of reasons: because she was so deeply devout. And since she and her order provided medical treatment, Hitchens's critique of her may apply to Dr. Driver as well.

Hitchens is indignant that despite Teresa's great reputation among the fashionably philanthropic of the world, she was not in fact a humanitarian. For had she been one, she would have been a modern, pain-relieving, oblivion dispensing medical practitioner, and would have trained her Sisters of Charity to be likewise, but she wasn't and she didn't.

Hitchens is of course correct; a modern medical practitioner Mother Teresa never claimed to be. I quote her: "We are first of all religious. We are not social workers, not teachers, not nurses or doctors. We are religious sisters. We serve Jesus in the poor. We nurse him, feed him, clothe him, visit him, comfort him in the poor, the abandoned, the sick, the orphans, the dying. Our lives are very much woven with the Eucharist. We have a deep faith in Jesus' Blessed Sacrament. Because of this faith, it is not so difficult to see Christ and touch him in the distressing disguise of the poor."

Now this is very powerful and wholly alien to the conception of medicine that prevails in the contemporary "agnostic academic workplace." It stands to it in the relation of charity to mere humanitarianism, but it must be recognized that the latter arose in opposition to the former with the intention of subverting and supplanting it. Compassion, like most social phenomena, is as important for what it isn't as for what it is. The crucial thing it isn't —what those great geniuses who launched it into the world in the 18th Century specifically designed it not to be—is Christian charity. Dr. Driver grasps this clearly; it's why she speaks of having to swim upstream in her agnostic academic workplace.

But if Mother Teresa remains our example —and again I apologize to Dr. Driver if she finds the comparison embarrassing—what she provided was not only more than a secular physician would—in addition to it but compatible with it—but irreconcilably different from it. Her approach to her patients was not primarily a clinical one, directed to healing their bodies or, that failing, to minimize their pain. As a practitioner of charity, she addressed the problem of suffering differently than if she were acting from compassion.

Indeed, even to recognize suffering as a problem (as opposed to merely an evil) is to step outside the bounds of the modern therapeutic mentality. Dr. Driver recounts of her early years as a physician that "each one of us ultimately faced the questions, 'Why am I doing this? What is the meaning of my patient's suffering? What is the value of my work?'" I wonder, however, how many of Dr. Driver's colleagues joined her in raising the question of the meaning of suffering. For the modern humanitarian, suffering exists to be abolished, and for no other reason. Like death itself, it is a natural defect, an objection to life. Only for the believer is suffering a problem, which is to say a riddle and an opportunity. As Teresa put it, "Suffering in itself is nothing, but suffering shared with Christ's passion is a wonderful gift to human life. Suffering is a sign of love because this is how God the Father proved that he loved the world — by giving his Son to die for us and expiate our sin. Suffering in itself does not bring joy, but Christ as seen in suffering does."

Hitchens's *Kulturkampf* against Mother Teresa dramatizes the clash between the Christian notion of salvation through suffering and the post-Christian project of the abolition of earthly suffering. So my question to Dr. Driver is simply this. Does this clash haunt her efforts to negotiate her agnostic academic workplace in the footsteps of St. Josemaria? Does she understand the Christian component of her medical practice as in addition to what her colleagues provide, or as in tension with it? Does her deep Christian faith, in sanctifying her working life, also greatly complicate it?

I turn now to the remarks of Carlos Cavallé. While so different from Dr. Driver's personal confession, his talk too evoked my admiration. What an idea not only to set out to ennoble the world of business through the example of St Josemaria but to conduct empirical research into the feasibility of this project. (I should add that I was privileged to enjoy a delightful conversation with Professor Cavallé yesterday afternoon in which he further expounded his project to me.) Where there's a will there's a way, much of the time, at least, and Professor Cavallé's will seems indomitable.

From one workplace to another, from the world of modern medicine to that of the modern commercial enterprise. Here too, we confront an audacious attempt to Christianize the designedly un-Christian. For as modern humanitarianism was the project of defectors from Christianity who had learned from it the better to supplant it, so modern economics was the creature of other thinkers (or even of the same ones) who conceived of it as furthering this same project. When we read Locke or Montesquieu, or Adam Smith — to cite just the three greatest theoretical proponents of a new world of commerce — we find a radical critique of Christian charity as having issued inevitably in economic stagnation. All three thinkers promoted the "invisible hand" of human self-interest —Smith's famous term— as superior to Christian principles in its effectiveness as a motivator and therefore in its tendency to promote the general welfare. They deemed greed to be good, not because they were lacking in philanthropic concern, but because they were guided by it. If there was to be boundless increase in the stock of goods available to sustain the human race, there must be boundless incentive to strive for it, and for this the only reliable motive was personal profit, liberated from the constraining shackles of Christian doctrine.

Well, it worked, productivity having soared to levels of which Locke and Smith could only have dreamed. Professor Cavallé welcomes this outcome: he is not anti-growth but pro-development. Nor is he simply hostile to the acquisitive passions. He does not malign ambition for oneself or on behalf of one's shareholders. He insists that the teachings of St. Josemaria do not override but even re-enforce "legitimate motives" of this sort. He is aware, however, that once liberated from the salutary restraints of the Christian faith, these motives tend to excess. As he himself puts it, we live today with "the imbalances that result from a materialistic approach to business and from personal and institutional greed."

Viewed from the perspective of the fathers of the modern economic enterprise, Dr. Cavallé seeks to reconfine this enterprise within that strait jacket of Christian doctrine its escape from which first defined it as modern and economic. Why do I state the matter in these loaded terms? Not because I am adverse to Professor Cavallé's project, any more than I am to Dr. Driver's, on the contrary, I wish him all success. But I want to raise the question of whether the synthesis for which he hopes —in which charity and acquisitiveness walk hand and hand— is as feasible as it would be desirable.

In conclusion, then, let me summarize my doubts about both these worthy projects, that of Dr. Driver and that of Professor Cavallé. As a student of the history of political thought, I'm convinced that modernity arose in the world in repudiation of Christianity, and that this repudiation was of its essence. Its founders aspired to a non-Christian future much brighter than the Christian past. Such was the ethos of their project and such has its ethos remained. From the point of view of Christianity, modernity is a runaway train. As for the workplace, it is the forge of modernity. There the systematic remaking of God's former world is incessantly advanced and consolidated. St Josemaria's "sanctification of work" is thus a project of breathtaking boldness. It would refound the modern edifice on the basis of the stone that the builders rejected.

Jenny Driver's Reply

I promise I'll be very brief. First, I want to ask for a copy of your remarks, so I can work on my homework after I get home.

I was extremely anxious when I was accepted to the program at Harvard because I thought that perhaps my devout Christian beliefs would be in terrible conflict with my academic community and then I really wouldn't make it. I'm certain that if I had been more up front about my beliefs regarding medical ethics I would not have been accepted. But I wasn't asked about them so I didn't talk about them.

But afterwards it was very interesting. I work in a Jewish hospital, the Beth Israel Hospital, for which I'm very, very grateful for many reasons. When it became obvious that I did have beliefs about health care ethics that were different from the "party line" that some people hold in the academic community at Harvard, there was support for me because of the history of the hospital. It was founded by people with strong religious beliefs who wanted to be cared for in a way that was in keeping with those beliefs, in a society that was in conflict with some of them. So I was respected and was even asked to become the chief resident, even though throughout my career there I did not prescribe contraception and I did not refer patients for abortion. Working that out within that system was really kind of an act of God. So, in fact it wasn't as much of a conflict as I thought it would be.

To the question whether Christianity really fits into the working environment there, I would say, yes, it fits in because that's what's missing. And in my experience of talking to colleagues who are agnostic, they actually admire what a person who does have religious beliefs brings to the profession, because I can tell you that when someone is dying in a hospital room, the more common approach is for physicians and health staff to walk by the room and not feel comfortable going in. My faith allows me to want to go in—that's the first place I want to go. That's the kind of thing that's missing, and so I would say that it's been embraced by my colleagues rather than rejected.

Carlos Cavallé's Reply

Thank you very much for your comments. In a recent book. one of the most distinguished philosophers alive makes the point that the contemporary world lacks a deep study of what a human person is. He says we are a hundred years behind in research on the nature of the human person. Research of this kind could help resolve the problem you raise..

I had the opportunity of living with this philosopher for a number of years and one day I told him, "Look, I have discussed current economic approaches with my colleagues around the world. If I go, for example, to the Harvard Business School, which is the epitome of liberal capitalism, and discuss these approaches with the Dean, we end up with the concept of the human person." So I asked my philosopher friend, "Can you give me a very simple way of explaining to other people who are not philosophers what a human person is?" A couple of months later he said, "I've got it!" Well, I can tell you what he said, but I cannot explain it in detail here and now. It would take much longer. But he said, "We know from experience and from revelation that the human person is a free and rational being created to the image and likeness of God. We know it." But then he added, "With an immortal soul that is longing for God." That is to say, we have a built-in capacity that makes our immortal soul long for God. It is not something that has been added to us. Any person in the world, in any corner of the world, has this built-in capacity. You cannot keep God away from business because then you keep a very important part of the individual person away from business, and then the person cannot fully realize himself in business.

The philosopher continued, "The human person is a rational and free individual, created in the image and likeness of God; and God has left His imprint so to speak in the human creature, giving the creature a built-in capacity which is a longing for God—and a built-in capacity to love others for themselves and not for selfish reasons." Now for a number of years, Adam Smith and your friends (and my friends) have been treating the human person in organizations as a resource, a *resource*, and even sometimes as a less important resource than coal, petrol, energy and other similar things. Well, they never got rid of material energy but they could get rid of people when they were not useful to them.

All this is changing because, even though we lack that hundred years of research on what the human person is, the world is beginning to realize that the materialistic approach to business that you described, which discards religion, is the wrong one. As you were telling me the other day, your father in his business used to act as a Jew. Modern economic theory is beginning to recognize the importance of the human person. An understanding of the human person is needed in order to make the human person the center of economic activity and not simply a natural resource or simply the market, the abstract market in general, as in the past. This is what is really needed, and I believe that the contribution of St. Josemaria in this respect is very important, because for him, there is nothing more important, after God, than the human person.

CECILIA A. ROYALS

LET THEM VIGOROUSLY CONTRIBUTE THEIR EFFORT:[1]
OPUS DEI AND THE NEW EVANGELIZATION

Introduction

The National Institute of Womanhood is a non-partisan, non-sectarian, civil-society organization that works to meet social challenges by promoting con-

Graeme Hunter, John Hartley, John Murphy, and Cecilia Royals at St. Michael's College, University of Toronto, January 10, 2003.

structive dialogue on issues pertaining to the development of the person, the family, and society through public opinion, policy analysis, and leadership development. It is incorporated in the State of Maryland, is governed by a constitution and a board of directors. It is a free and autonomous social entity.

Neither the Catholic Church nor Opus Dei directs the activities of NIW. Any suggestion of such a link would be a throw-back to a distorted understanding of the laity, when the laity were limited to participating in the apostolic activities of the hierarchy. The autonomy and freedom of NIW to function in the world as it sees fit, not linked to Opus Dei or the Church, are precisely what demonstrate a very important element of Opus Dei and the dynamism of the new evangelization.

---

[1] Second Vatican council, Dogmatic Constitution on the Church, *LumenGentium*, 36.

I have experienced Opus Dei from the inside. I have been a supernumerary member since 1982. However, I do not claim to represent Opus Dei or to speak for it. I have also experienced the Church from the inside. I am a cradle Catholic and have endeavored to be faithful all my life. However, I neither claim to represent the Church nor to speak for it. I speak for myself and mine and act for myself and mine. My decisions are mine to make and mine to follow through with and mine to be responsible for. I am a free and autonomous person. I am a lay person. As a lay person I strive to live my vocation faithfully. Sometimes that striving is covered up with a lot of ashes; the engine is barely running. Other times, the engine is bright and shiny and full of energy.

In *Evangelii Nuntiandi*, Pope Paul VI explains the role of lay people in the new evangelization:

> Lay people, whose particular vocation places them in the midst of the world and *in charge* of the most varied temporal tasks, must for this very reason exercise a very special form of evangelization...
>
> Their own field of evangelizing activity is the vast and complicated world of politics, society and economics, but also the world of culture, of the sciences and the arts, of international life, of the mass media. It also includes other realities which are open to evangelization, such as human love, the family, the education of children and adolescents, professional work, suffering.[2]

The universal call to holiness and the consequent implications for the laity at the heart of the "new evangelization" resonate completely with the central teaching of Opus Dei. It is this resonance and the recognition of the dignity, autonomy, and freedom of the laity to vigorously contribute their efforts to the building of the kingdom that link in my person Opus Dei, the new evangelization, and The National Institute of Womanhood.

New Evangelization

Let me now offer what I have gleaned from church documents about the laity with regard to the new evangelization. This new evangelization is not a new program, but a new era imbued with a special dynamism. Again in the words of Pope Paul VI, it is "a fresh forward impulse, capable of creating within a Church still more firmly rooted in the undying power and strength of Pentecost a new period of evangelization."[3] This new period remains faithful "both to a message whose servants we are and to the people to whom we must transmit it living and intact."[4] It is what it has always been from apostolic times, "the proclamation of Christ by word and the testimony of life."[5] Pope Paul was careful to warn against a partial or fragmentary understanding of this evange-

---

[2] Paul VI, Apostolic Exhortation, *Evangelii Nuntiandi*, 70.

[3] *Evangelii Nuntiandi, 2.*

[4] *Evangelii Nuntiandi, 4.*

[5] *Catechism of the Catholic Church*, New York, 1994, 905.

lization which may even distort or impoverish "all its richness, complexity and dynamism."[6]

The special dynamism draws its energy from the exhortation, born out of the Second Vatican Council, especially in *Lumen Gentium, Gaudium et Spes*, and *Ad Gentes,* that *all* the faithful, through holiness of life, should imbue culture and human activity with the spirit of Christ. This exhortation underscores the awareness that *the laity have the principal role* in this transformation of culture and human activity: "Therefore, by their competence in secular training and by their activity, elevated from within by the grace of Christ, let them vigorously contribute their effort, so that created goods may be perfected by human labor, technical skill and civic culture for the benefit of all men according to the design of the Creator and the light of His Word."[7]

Pope John Paul II emphasized this point in his apostolic letter *Tertio Millennio Adveniente*, saying that the new evangelization "opened up broad areas for the participation of the laity.... [And] is an expression of the strength which Christ has given to the entire People of God."[8]

Opus Dei and the New Evangelization

The universal call to holiness and the consequent implications for the laity at the heart of the 'new evangelization' echo the central teaching of Opus Dei, that the laity should participate in its own way in the mission of Christ and his Church. In the words of Saint Josemaria: "The sole objective of Opus Dei has always been to see to it that there be men and women of all races and social conditions who endeavor to love and to serve God and the rest of mankind in and through their ordinary work, in the midst of the realities and interests of the world."[9]

The implication of this spiritual emancipation is that ordinary persons are no longer restricted by customs, traditions and distorted concepts of the laity. It is an extraordinary breakthrough for the average person to have these paths opened. These paths of heroic virtue and extraordinary professionalism in ordinary work, implied in the universal call to sanctity, explode the limits previously imposed on the laity. Henceforth, we are to become men and woman of integrity, capable of "serving [our] fellow citizens and contributing to the solutions of the great problems of mankind."[10]

Autonomy and Freedom

Persons everywhere are becoming increasingly aware of the fact that they too are meant to reach for the pinnacles of human achievement, in and through their ordinary activities. Not only are we truly free, autonomous, and responsi-

---

[6] *Evangelii Nuntiandi*, 17.

[7] *LumenGentium*, 36.

[8] John Paul II, Apostolic Letter. *Tertio Millennio Adveniente*, 21.

[9] *Conversations with Mgr. Escriva de Balaguer*, 10.

[10] *Christ is Passing By*, 28.

ble for our own actions, but we are also encouraged to take actions that are bold, broad, and strong.

St. Josemaria expressed it this way:

> Personal freedom is essential to the Christian life. But do not forget, my children, that I always speak of a responsible freedom. Interpret, then, my words as what they are: a call to exercise your rights every day, and not merely in time of emergency. A call to fulfill honorably your commitments as citizens, in all fields — in politics and in financial affairs, in university life and in your job — accepting with courage all the consequences of your free decisions and the personal independence which corresponds to each one of you.[12]

The influence of St. Josemaria on my life has been radical. He has touched the core of my being and explained to me the purpose of my existence. He has taught me to love work as an offering to God, united to the sacrifice of the mass, for my sanctification and the sanctification of the whole world. He has taught me to desire to do it to the best of my capacity for the glory of God and in order for it to be an offering worthy of God. He has taught me to love ordinary work, to devote the time and study necessary to increase my effectiveness. Gradually, I have learned to extend and expand my work, not shrink it. To do more, better, faster.

His influence led me to extend and expand my work from the confines of my family to encompass the greater community. His exhortation to "*fearlessly... strive to play a part in the human developments and decisions on which the present and future of society depend*"[13] propelled me, along with a handful of women and men, to organize The National Institute of Womanhood. The propelling comes from Opus Dei. The wind in the sails is from St. Josemaria. In the words of St. Josemaria "all the activity of [Opus Dei] is directed fundamentally to one task: to provide the members with the spiritual assistance necessary for their life of piety, and an adequate spiritual, doctrinal, religious, and human formation. And then, off you go!"[14] Off we go to use our talents and initiative freely and responsibly for the service of God and our neighbor according to what we can see and can conjure up. Off we go as autonomous persons making use of our grit to exercise our special form of evangelization. Which is, in the words of Paul VI, "affecting and as it were upsetting, through the power of the Gospel, mankind's criteria of judgment, determining values, points of interest, lines of thought, sources of inspiration and models of life."[15]

The autonomy and freedom of NIW to affect lines of thought, to function in the world as it sees fit, not directed by Opus Dei or the Church, are precisely what demonstrate a very important element of Opus Dei and the dynamism

---

[12] *Passionately Loving the World,,* 117.

[13] *Forge,* 715.

[14]*Conversations,* 19.

[15] *Evangelii Nuntiandi,* 19.

of the new evangelization. That is: the element of trusting the laity to transform man's culture—and allowing the laity to do so.

Examples from The National Institute of Womanhood

NIW competes, like many other organizations, for a voice in the market place of ideas, where it vigorously contributes its efforts for the improvement of society. NIW is a pro-active think tank that has participated in key United Nations events such as The International Conference on Population and Development (ICPD) in Cairo, September, 1994; The Fourth World Conference on Women in Beijing, September, 1995; and The Summit on the Rights of the Child in 2002. The Institute has testified before the United States Senate Foreign Relations Committee, addressed the United Nations Commission of the Status of Women, addressed international conferences in North and South America and Europe, and hosted an international Conference in Beijing. Currently, NIW hosts a web site,[16] continues to monitor the United Nations on social issues, sponsors roundtables and conferences, and speaks to the media on issues pertinent to its mission.

NIW held an international conference on the crisis in the understanding of womanhood in Huairou, China. The event was extremely well attended, standing room only. Over 60 countries were represented among the participants. A contingent from the Lesbian Caucus came prepared to dispute with the panelists. The tension was apparent, but as the representatives of NIW expressed NIW's understanding of woman the tension noticeably left the room. A member of the Lesbian Caucus remarked during the question and answer period, "I have to admit that I am surprised to find that you are pro-woman." Later the leader of the Lesbian Caucus, after questioning, one-on-one, an NIW panelist, was moved and asked, "Is there a place in your organization for a woman like me?"

Affecting or, perhaps, upsetting, through the power of sound ideas the lines of thought of these women and other men and women around the globe is the work of NIW. It is up front and spelled out in our mission. We work hard to articulate what is true and enduring about woman.

Following the 4th World Conference of Women in Beijing, the Chinese government sent a delegation of over twenty-five women to the US to learn about non-governmental organizations. NIW was selected along with several other organizations. The women who attended NIW's workshop had many years of experience in the Communist Party and were leaders of major labor organizations. Our information packet included the following introductory paragraph:

> The National Institute of Womanhood calls on women of vision to take the cultural domain, women of character who can mold from our heritage the cornerstones of a new culture that will enrich and ennoble all its people. The time has come to define anew our cultural ethos, in order to secure a society that

---

[16] www.uniw.org

honors its women, and to build a civilization in which the human person can flourish.

Via a simultaneous translator we shared with them our vision of woman and answered many of their questions. And then something unusual happened. They erupted into a lively discussion amongst themselves in Chinese. The translator eagerly explained to us that the women were admitting to each other that NIW's concept of woman was what each had believed about woman; but each had been under the impression she was the only one who thought that way. The translator explained that these women, who were communist philosophers, were, for the first time, having a conversation among themselves about this subject.

In 1994 NIW was the only organization to testify before the Senate Foreign Relations Committee against the ratification of a treaty that NIW considers to be against women and against mothers. Subsequent to that testimony many other US organizations have come out openly and testified against the treaty.

We publish a newsletter that is sent to every state in the nation and reaches over 1800 leaders across the US. It not only reaches local organizations, but also ministers of many denominations, college professors, youth leaders, and heads of families.

Conclusion

I have shown in general terms that the approach of Opus Dei to the new evangelization is consonant with the recent exhortations of the Church to the laity. In particular, I have explained my contribution to the new evangelization, as a lay, supernunumerary woman, through my work with The National Institute of Womanhood.

JOHN K. MURPHY

OPUS DEI AND THE NEW EVANGELIZATION

Introduction

The founder of *Opus Dei*, Saint Josemaria Escriva, was a modern apostle who was moved by God's grace and brought to the world a message of great novelty for its time: in his own words "as old as the Gospel and, like the Gospel, new." It is a message that reminds us that we are called to be "not just *alter Christus,* but *ipse Christus",* Christ himself, in our families, in our professional work and in the ordinary circumstances of our lives.

This message was indeed a foreshadowing of things to come as a very concerned Pope John XXIII convoked the Second Vatican Council in an effort to bring the Church to express her teachings in contemporary language because of what he perceived to be a crisis in society. Blessed Pope John XXIII felt that society was evolving in such a way as to exclude God and that every effort had to be made to render the Good News more readily understood and ensure that society was penetrated with "the vivifying and perennial energies of the Gospel."[1] The Council Fathers determined that the most effective way for this to happen would be to mobilize the laity in the task of evangelization.[2] As a result, a renewed theology of mission and evangelization emerged from the Council whereby all Christ's faithful not only have the obligation to spread "the divine message of salvation," they have the right to do so.[3]

As the divide between faith and culture has grown during the intervening years, especially in the West, Pope John Paul II has repeatedly called the faithful to embrace a pastoral vision that he calls the "new evangelization." In his post-synodal apostolic exhortation *Ecclesia in America,*[4] the Holy Father outlined many elements for thought and action on the part of all believers. He drew special attention to the challenge of evangelizing in urban centres, the cities. He says "just as she was able to evangelize rural culture for centuries, the Church is called in the same way today to undertake a methodical and far-reaching urban evangelization."[5]

---

[1] *Humanae Salutis*, 3
[2] cf. Second Vatican Council, *Lumen gentium* no. 33, *Apostolicam acuositatem* no. 25
[3] cf. Code of Canon Law, can. 211
[4] *The Church in America,* Jan. 22, 1999 (Hereinafter *EA*)
[5] *EA*, 21

The recent synod drew attention to the need for a new urban evangelization through catechesis, liturgy and the pastoral structures. Their objective is to "look towards a fresh and more profound experience of community in Christ, which is the only effective and enduring response to a culture of rootlessness, anonymity and inequality."[6] Where this experience is weak, the Pope says, "we may expect more of the faithful to lose interest in religion or drift into the sects and pseudo-religious groups which feed off alienation and which flourish among Christians who are disenchanted with the Church for one reason or another."[7] The Holy Father cautions that "we can no longer expect people to come spontaneously to our communities: the Church must seek out people."[8]

What the synod called for is nothing short of the evangelization which the Pope described as "new in ardour, methods and expression."[9] He stressed the role of the parish in this "new evangelization," saying that it remained the "privileged place" for meeting Jesus and for the liturgical life "centred on the real presence of Christ in the Eucharist, which is the unchangeable truth of the Christian life and service for the spiritual richness of the Church." He called for new methods and new structures to be found in parishes "to build bridges between persons." The Holy Father mentioned also that schools and other institutions of the Church must also open themselves to leading people to Christ and free themselves from "influences linked to secularization."

During his life and priestly ministry, Saint Josemaria had already undertaken this project of the "new evangelization" while, perhaps, not calling it such. Animated with the zeal that one finds in saints, he did not limit himself to proclaiming the Good News in word alone. By the grace of God, *Opus Dei* was founded on October 2, 1928. Saint Josemaria began a specific and effective way of carrying out God's universal salvific will: a "way of sanctification in daily work and in the fulfillment of the Christian's ordinary duties." In his address to members of *Opus Dei* on January 12, 2002, Pope John Paul II stated that "the Lord gives to every baptized person the grace necessary to reach the summit of divine charity. The small events of each day hold, locked with them, an unsuspected greatness. Those actions, undertaken with the love of God and neighbour, can overcome at their very root every division between faith and daily life."

It is sanctification, the quest for sanctification, the way of sanctification, that is at the root of the Christian vocation.[10] The work of Saint Josemaria has given structure and direction to so many in the quest for what is most essential in the human person, holiness itself. In the words of Pope John Paul II,

---

[6]*Evangelization of Urban Culture Is a Formidable Challenge for the Church*, Ad Limina Address to Bishops from Ontario, Canada (on May 4, 1999) - no.4

[7]*Ibid.*

[8]*Ibid.*

[9]*Address* to the Bishops of CELAM (March 9,1983), III: *Insegnamenti*, VI, 1 (1983), 698.

[10]cf. Vatican I, *Lumen gentium*, 39-42

"Moreover, by sanctifying one's work in accord with the norms of objective reality, the lay faithful contribute in an effective way to building up a society that is more worthy of man."[11]

Opus Dei and the "New Evangelization"

Today I want to discuss the link between the work of *Opus Dei* and the pastoral vision of Pope John Paul II, specifically what he calls the "new evangelization." On the Solemnity of the Epiphany of the Lord, following the ceremony for the closing of the Holy Door at St. Peter's Basilica, the Holy Father signed the Apostolic Letter *Novo Millennio Ineunte*.[12] The document addresses the basic question that many of us pondered after the celebration of the Great Jubilee: "Where do we go from here?" The Holy Father urges us to go forth: "*Duc in altum!*" He calls us to "put out into the deep" in obedience to the command given by Jesus to the apostle Peter. The Church, by going to deeper water, is called to undertake the challenges of the future.

Pope John Paul II is clear in his letter that meeting Christ is the legacy of the Great Jubilee. He thanks God for the principal events that highlighted this year of grace. He recalls the great ecumenical beginning in St. Paul's Basilica with the leaders of different religions, the powerful act of "purification of memory," his pilgrimage to the Holy Land, and the ongoing call to mission.

Beyond the wonderful and memorable external events, Pope John Paul II views the Great Jubilee above all as an event of grace, confident that it has touched countless people's lives and has called them to undertake a journey of ever deeper conversion to the Lord. A renewed meeting with Christ is the Jubilee's true legacy, one which must now be treasured and invested for the future.

This new millennium means "starting afresh from Christ," and it can't be stressed enough that all of our pastoral activity must have as its goal an experience of solid faith, leading to "the universal call to holiness." That is why we are gathered here today. As Saint Josemaria affirmed again and again, it is with holiness as our goal that we seek to proclaim Christ and his teachings in all that we say and do. The Prelature of *Opus Dei* strives to be a faithful witness to Christ's call to serve, always in ways that are animated by unity and charity. But I am not here to tell you about *Opus Dei*, you know the life of the Prelature better than I. However, as I continue to speak about the "new evangelization" I am asking you to situate *Opus Dei*, to situate yourself, within the context of this exciting pastoral vision.

In his letter outlining the Church's hopes for the third millennium, Pope John Paul II encourages us to go to deeper waters in fidelity to the Gospel. He exhorts us to leave behind the tranquil waters that harbour the comforts of our lives, and launch out courageously into all the seas of the world, in the "new

---

[11] Jan. 12th, 2002

[12] *Beginning the New Millennium,* January 6th 2001 (Hereinafter *NMI*)

evangelization" of society. It is no accident that the Lord has raised up *Opus Dei* to fish for souls, obedient to the Lord's command: "Put out into the deep and let down your nets for a catch."[13] It seems to me that *Opus Dei* is ideally suited to carry out the task of the "new evangelization" whereby the faithful of the Prelature bring the Gospel to the various sectors of society in which they live and work. *Opus Dei*, with its essentially secular spirit, serves the Church and society by fostering individual holiness and apostolic commitment among the faithful, helping them to discover and take on the demands of their Christian vocation in the specific places they occupy in the world.

Novo Millennio Ineunte

Novo Millennio Ineunte culminates the drafting of a pastoral plan which has been in the works since Karol Wojtyla was elected to the Chair of Peter in 1978. In this document the Holy Father calls us to be "witnesses to love," and reflects upon "communion" as the key term for understanding the mystery of the Church.[14] He identifies several indispensable commitments that we must focus on:

(1) Ecumenism: so that with all our brothers and sisters in faith we may live more and more of the full unity which the Church already enjoys in Christ.[15]

(2) Fraternal charity: Pope John Paul II says that many challenges face the Church, impelling her to become, with still greater imagination and generosity, an expression of God's concrete love in the countless situations of human suffering and poverty. He speaks of the courageous witness to which Christians are called in every area of social and cultural life, especially the family, the protection of life, the ecological crisis, and unethical scientific experimentation.[16]

(3) Interreligious dialogue: without in any way diminishing the need for Christian proclamation, dialogue remains an important sign post for everyone in advancing the search for truth and the promotion of peace.[17]

This is, in a nutshell, the Holy Father's agenda for the new millennium and the "new evangelization" is at its very core.

What is the "new evangelization"?

In order to speak about the "new evangelization" we must first be clear on what is meant by the term. The term "new evangelization" was first used by Pope John Paul II on March 9th 1983 in a speech to the Latin American bishops in Port-au-Prince, Haiti. He made it clear to them (CELAM) that the 500th anniversary of Christopher Columbus' arrival in the Americas, to be commemorated in 1992, required "a commitment, not to re-evangelization, but to a new evangelization, new in ardour, methods and expression."

---

[13]Lk. 5:4

[14]*NMI*, 43

[15]*NMI*, 48

[16]*NMI*, 49

[17]*NMI*, 55

On December 7th 1990 Pope John Paul II issued the encyclical *Redemptoris Missio* (Mission of the Redeemer) in which he distinguished the "new evangelization" from the Church's traditional form of evangelization which is aimed at "persons or groups who do not yet believe in Christ...and whose culture has not yet been influenced by the Gospel".[18] He made the clarification that the "new evangelization" is rather directed to situations "where entire groups of the baptized have lost a living sense of the faith, or even no longer consider themselves members of the Church, and live a life far removed from Christ and his Gospel."[19]

It is important to note that the seeds of the "new evangelization" have been present for some time. Indeed they were already present in Pope John XXIII's decision to convoke the Second Vatican Council. In his speech opening the Council in 1962, the Blessed Pope John XXIII declared that "the greatest concern of the ecumenical council is this: that the sacred deposit of Christian doctrine should be guarded and taught more efficaciously." Not letting the matter rest, in 1974 his successor Pope Paul VI convoked a synod of bishops to address the topic and this resulted in the post-synodal apostolic exhortation *Evangelii Nuntiandi.* Evidently Pope John Paul II has made evangelization, and specifically the "new evangelization," a very high priority in his papacy. He has forged a deep connection between the "new evangelization" and the arrival of the third millennium. The preparation for the Great Jubilee was in fact the unfolding of a profound pastoral plan preparing the Church's faithful to embrace this task. The Holy Father gave voice to a deep sense of urgency and made it abundantly clear in his letter of November 10th 1994 entitled *Tertio Millennio Advenientes* (The Coming of the Third Millennium). He stated in stark terms that "the more the West is becoming estranged from its Christian roots, the more it is becoming missionary territory."[20]

Remembering the Great Jubilee

While we reflect upon that statement, let's take some time to reflect back on the Jubilee Year and what led up to it. On Christmas Eve of 1999 in St. Peter's Basilica, Pope John Paul II opened the Holy Door thus marking the beginning of the Great Jubilee of the year 2000. Like so many popes before him dating back to the 15th century, John Paul II stood before the Holy Door, and the Church stood with him in prayer, in silence, and recollection to begin this year of God's favour, a year of grace, a year to devote ourselves more fervently to the spiritual journey of faith.

After the door was opened the choir sang an acclamation: *"Christus heri et hodie, finis et principium, Christus alpha et omega, ipsi gloria in saecula!"* "Christ yesterday and today, the end and the beginning, the alpha and the

---

[18]*Redemptoris Missio,* 34 (Hereinafter *RM*)

[19]*RM,* 33

[20]*Tertio Millennio Adveniente,* 57 (Hereinafter *TMA*)

omega, to him be glory forever." This short acclamation really provides a synthesis of the "new evangelization", what it is, what it is about, what the door is, and who and what it opens to.

With all the talk of the new millennium, all the predictions, and prognostications about the future, the opening of the Holy Door reminded us that the future and the end are not about a time or even a place—but a person, Jesus Christ, and a personal God—Father, Son and Holy Spirit. It is into the life of this mystery, a personal mystery, that we have been introduced, by name, at the moment of our Baptism.

The Responsibility of Every Believer to "Cross the Threshold"

With the opening of the Holy Door the Church reminded us of "the responsibility of every believer to cross its threshold" in faith and in hope.[21] The Church reminded us that it is not enough that the Holy Father opened the door on Christmas eve. That was only the beginning. What remains for all of us is to respond to the invitation—each and every one of us—to cross this threshold, to enter the door that symbolizes Christ: "I am the gate. Whoever enters by me will be saved, and will come in and go out and find pasture."[22]

The period of the "new evangelization" is a time of the Lord's favour, a time of grace, a time of celebration, a time to deepen our faith, a time to strive toward unity, and so the importance of dialogue with other religions. The importance of being reconciled with others was demonstrated so clearly and powerfully by the Pope's pilgrimage to the Holy Land. The "new evangelization" is a time to make a positive step ahead on the journey of faith. Easily said, but to do so we can't bring all our baggage with us. We need to give something up. We need to leave something behind. What is it?

Understanding the Jubilee

If we are honest with ourselves and each other, the Great Jubilee can give us some sobering insights into just what we must leave behind if our efforts in the "new evangelization" are to be an authentic witness to the Gospel. The word "jubilee" comes from the hebrew *yobel,* or *yovel,* which means "ram's horn," or "trumpet". The Latin *jubilaeus,* from the verb *jubilare,* signifies the sounding of the trumpet which accompanies the Holy Year devoted to the Lord. In fact, according to the 25th Chapter of the Book of Leviticus, every seven years Israel was to observe the Sabbath year when the land was allowed to rest, a year in which all debts were cancelled and those who had become slaves were to be freed. All of this was done in honour of God.[23]

The Holy Father develops this aspect of Jubilee when he states that the "...Jubilee Year was meant to restore equality among all the children of Israel,

---

[21] *Incarnationis mysterium,* 8
[22] John 10:9
[23] *TMA,* 12

offering new possibilities to families which had lost their property and even their personal freedom. On the other hand, the Jubilee Year was a reminder to the rich that a time would come when their Israelite slaves would once again be their equals and would be able to reclaim their rights."[24] We should note that the prescriptions for the Jubilee set out in the 25th Chapter of Leviticus remained ideals, more hopes than things that were ever carried out in actual fact. These things remain great challenges for us as we cross the threshold of the third millennium and embrace the "new evangelization".

While the custom of the Jubilee begins in the Old Testament, it continues in the history of the Church and is key to her future. In Luke 4:16-30 Jesus stands up in the synagogue at Capernaum and reads Isaiah 61:1-2: "The Spirit of the Lord God is upon me, because the Lord has anointed me; he has sent me to bring good news to the oppressed, to bind up the brokenhearted, to proclaim liberty to the captives, and release to the prisoners; to proclaim the year of the Lord's favour."

When Jesus said that "today these words have been fulfilled in your hearing",[25] he indicated that he is the long-awaited Messiah foretold in the prophets, and that the "long-awaited time" was beginning in him. In Jesus the day of salvation has come, in Jesus the fulness of time has arrived. For the Church the Jubilee points to the time of the Messiah, to the mission of Christ.

The Great Jubilee in the writings of Pope John Paul II

Since the publication of his very first encyclical *Redemptor Hominis* (The Redeemer of Man) on March 4th 1979, Pope John Paul II has continued to speak of the Great Jubilee of the year 2000. In particular he suggested that the years leading up to the year 2000 be lived as "a new Advent."[26] The years of preparation for the Jubilee were placed by the Holy Father under the sign of the most Holy Trinity: through Christ—in the Holy Spirit—to God the Father.

With the publication of *Tertio Millennio Adveniente* in 1994, the Holy Father renewed now in somewhat more urgent tones his calls in earlier writings to contemplate the mystery of God under the mystery of the Holy Trinity during the years leading up to the Jubilee. Both the Jubilee Year and devotion to the Blessed Trinity mark the papacy of John Paul II. The Holy Father states it himself when he says, "In fact, preparing for the year 2000 has become as it were a hermeneutical key of my pontificate".[27]

In the writings of Pope John Paul II we really need to pay attention to such expressions as "new Advent," "new springtime of Christianity," "new Pentecost," "new period of grace and mission," "the fullness of time," the call to discern "what the Spirit is saying to the churches." What is John Paul II try-

---

[24]*TMA*, 13

[25]Lk. 4:21

[26]*Redemptor Hominis*, 1

[27]*TMA*, 23

ing to tell us? At the very least such expressions should lead us to take this call to consider the importance of the "new evangelization" and to participate fully in this mission for our own spiritual good, for the good of the Church and for the good of humanity.

The Pope, in his calls to prepare for the new millennium has repeatedly emphasized that the year 2000 be approached as an important opportunity for a genuine encounter with the Trinitarian God, an encounter that takes place individually and collectively. The God that we encounter, the God that we celebrate is a personal God, God the Father, the Son and the Holy Spirit.

The importance of prayer in the "new evangelization"

There is a great danger that we become sidetracked and ignore this hidden treasure which is ours in prayer, the great mystery of the Kingdom of God which we are called to mediate to others through our words, deeds, in our very lives.

We would do well to look to the Gospels and to Jesus' own example of prayer. It is in prayer that Jesus hears and embraces the will of God. Jesus not only discerns the purposes of the Father in prayer, but states his willingness to follow the will of the Father.

The same idea appears to be at work in Lk. 6:12-16. Jesus "spent the night in prayer to God," prior to choosing the twelve. Jesus thus discerns the Father's purposes in prayer and, in prayer, puts his determinations into practice. As well, Jesus' divine commission received at his Baptism in the Jordan is associated by Luke with prayer.[28] As was said in the biography of Don Didimo, the parish priest of Bassan del Grappa, "Jesus preached by day, by night he prayed."

How should we approach the "new evangelization"?

The Holy Father has given us much to reflect upon, pray about and act upon as we embrace his vision for the new millennium and the "new evangelization". It is surely too much to absorb at once, or even over a lifetime. Joseph Cardinal Ratzinger, Prefect of the Congregation for the Doctrine of the Faith, in his address "The New Evangelization" given for the Jubilee of Catechists 2000, reflects on the structure, method and essential contents of the "new evangelization". His Eminence cautions us against being too ambitious, looking for results and success according to human standards: "the temptation of impatience, the temptation of immediately finding the great success, in finding large numbers." In terms of the structure of the "new evangelization", he says it "must surrender to the mystery of the grain of the mustard seed and not be so pretentious as to immediately produce a large tree."

In terms of the method, the Cardinal directs us to the very core of the Christian faith. He states that "the sign of the Son is his communion with the Father. The Son introduces us into the Trinitarian communion, into the circle of

---

[28]Lk 3:21

eternal love, whose persons are 'pure relations,' the pure act of giving oneself and of welcome. The Trinitarian plan—visible in the Son, who does not speak in his name—shows the form of life of the true evangelizer—rather, evangelizing is not merely a way of speaking, but a form of living: living in the listening and giving voice to the Father."

Cardinal Ratzinger focuses on the life and ministry of Jesus in listing the contents essential for "new evangelization." Very simply they are found in proclaiming conversion, the Kingdom of God, proclaiming Jesus Christ and proclaiming eternal life. He concludes his address by saying, "If we take the Christian message into well-thought-out consideration, we are not speaking of a whole lot of things. In reality, the Christian message is very simple: We speak about God and man, and in this way we say everything."

A Brief Summary of the "new evangelization"

1) We must first evangelize ourselves.

"We cannot evangelize if we do not first evangelize ourselves, if we are not personally an object of evangelization."

2) We cannot keep Christ for ourselves.

"Those who have come into genuine contact with Christ cannot keep Him for themselves; they must proclaim Him."[29]

3) Let people know that God loves them.

According to the Holy Father the first thing this "new evangelization" should announce is that "humanity is loved by God!"[30]

4) Christ is the programme.

Pope John Paul II is very clear that "It is not therefore a matter of inventing a 'new program.' The program already exists: it is the plan found in the Gospel and in the living tradition; it is the same as ever".[31]

5) We have to learn to pray, to learn the trinitarian shape of Christian prayer.

6) We must nourish ourselves with the Word to be servants of conversion.

Pope John Paul II explains: "Only someone who has been transformed by Christ's law of love (as seen from the Gospel) can bring about a true *metanoia* (conversion) in the hearts and minds of others, in the different fields of endeavour, in nations, in the world."[32]

7) Christian witness is love of neighbour, works of mercy.

Pope John Paul II acknowledges that actions speak louder than words: "The transformation (of man) thus becomes a source of the witness which the world is waiting for. It can be summed up, first of all in love of neighbor, in the works of mercy."

---

[29]*NMI*, 32

[30]*Christifideles Laici*, 34

[31]*NMI*, 29

[32]*NMI*, 40

8) We must live a spirituality of communion.

In *Novo Millennio Ineunte,* the Holy Father speaks of the need for every Christian to be formed in the life of the Gospel, summing it up in the new commandment of Jesus. He invites the entire People of God (from those at the apex of the institutional Church down to the last faithful), that people he had called since 1983 must bring about a "new evangelization," to live its necessary consequence, i.e., a "spirituality of communion."

9) The essential "newness" of ardour, methods and modes.

In 1988 the Holy Father explains these features and says that evangelization will be new in ardour if it gradually increases union with God in those who promote it. It will be new in methods if it is carried out by the entire People of God. It will be new in modes of expression if it is in conformity with the promptings of the Spirit.

10) The Gospel is directed not only at individuals but communities.

11) The role of the laity is essential.

"The laity have their part to fulfill in the formation of these ecclesial communities, not only through a testimony that only they can give (the *consecratio mundi* through the various fields of human endeavor) but also through a missionary zeal and activity towards the many people who still do not believe and who no longer live the faith received at Baptism."[33]

12) The New Pentecost is what we await in hope.

The Holy Father says that "we must rekindle in ourselves the impetus of the beginnings and allow ourselves to be filled with the ardour of the apostolic preaching which followed Pentecost." Commenting on the current situation he states that "even in countries evangelized many centuries ago, the reality of a 'Christian society' which, amid all the frailties which have always marked human life, measured itself explicitly on Gospel values, is now gone. Today we must courageously face a situation which is becoming increasingly diversified and demanding, in the context of 'globalization' and of the consequent new and uncertain mingling of peoples and cultures. (...) we must (therefore) revive in ourselves the burning conviction of Paul, who cried out: 'woe to me if I do not preach the Gospel!'"[34]

Conclusion

Pope John Paul II has challenged the universal Church with a renewed and life-giving vision of her future. The task of undertaking the challenge is one in which all believers share. *Opus Dei* has proven itself to have many willing and capable crew members as the Boat of Peter charts its course into the third millennium of Christianity and prepares to cast its nets into the deep. The Church is headed for new depths of Christian experience, taking its bearing from the stellar pastoral and mystical heritage of a two thousand year voyage. But we

---

[33]*Christifideles Laici,* 34
[34]1 Cor. 9:16

must pray. To leave an abundant catch at Christ's feet, to bring souls closer to God, we have to be in constant touch with God in prayer. Yes, personal prayer, but above all community prayer, starting with the Eucharist, "source and summit" of the Church's life.

Duc in altum! May the work founded by Saint Josemaria be an ever more efficacious instrument of the new apostolic outreach, inspired and sustained by confidence in the presence of Christ and the power of the Holy Spirit. Let us now joyfully prepare ourselves for what the Holy Father calls "a new Advent,"[35] "a new springtime of Christianity,"[36] "a New Pentecost," "a new period of grace and mission."[37]

Saint Josemaria Escriva, pray for us.

---

[35]*TMA*
[36] Ibid.
[37]*NMI*

GRAEME HUNTER

RESPONSE TO THE PAPERS BY CECILIA ROYALS AND MSGR. JOHN MURPHY

Mrs. Royals has vigorously defended the autonomy of the National Institute of Womanhood and its evangelical effectiveness, precisely on the grounds that it enjoys the freedom with which the best thought of Opus Dei and Vatican II entrusts the laity.

Msgr. Murphy stresses the novelty of the new evangelization, calling back to living faith those whose faith has grown cold (sometimes ourselves), the importance of prayer and parish, and of being centred on Christ in the spirit of the year of Jubilee.

In my comments I would like to raise some general questions about evangelization and Opus Dei that their comments leave open to discussion. Evangelization is a hot potato for contemporary Christians for two reasons: (1) It challenges multiculturalism. (2) It challenges the idea that the other churches (the Orthodox Churches) and the "ecclesial communities" (Protestant denominations) ought to be immune from evangelization. Opus Dei is committed to evangelization through ordinary life and therefore can be regarded as having to handle both these hot potatoes. I would like to say why, as a Protestant, I approve of what I understand to be Opus Dei's approach to both issues.

Multiculturalism

First, why is it good to challenge *multiculturalism*? There are 3 reasons:

First, the idea of "culture" at the core of multiculturalism is itself a mistake. Like so many bad things the notion of "culture" as we understand it today appeared first at the end of the eighteenth century. "Culture" originally meant cultivation, in the farmer's sense of the term. It was used for the first time in the romantic period to refer to those vague, but now familiar things: English culture, German culture, Eastern culture (or should that be Chinese culture, Indian culture ... ?) As is the way with vague terms, it turned out to be infinitely extendable. We soon learned to distinguish between high culture and low culture, between pop culture and classical culture etc. The core idea is this: Cultures are supposed to be historically determined ways of life that allegedly distinguish different groups of people and their offspring. Vague, vague, vague— to the point of uselessness. What do people mean—and there are many such people—who would claim simultaneously to belong to Canadian culture, pop culture, and Protestant or Catholic culture? Do they mean anything other than that they are Canadian, Protestants or Catholics who like pop music? If they mean anything else, I don't know what it is.

Why, then, has this term 'culture' become so prevalent? The answer is because at one time it had a use. At the time of the sudden rise in importance of the natural sciences in the seventeenth and eighteenth centuries, when the chattering classes of the day wanted to be able to identify their lofty thoughts with something less mechanical and reductive than the objects of physics and chemistry, in desperation they coined the word 'culture' in its new sense. The sciences dealt with material objects, but humanists like themselves envisioned higher things; they dealt with culture. 'L'homme machine', the human machine, may have suggested a fascinating program of study to people of a scientific cast of mind, but to those of humanist training it sounded like the death of the spirit, what C.S. Lewis would later call the abolition of man.

The word "culture" was also politically useful at that time. It gave focus to the rising nationalism of Western European countries. These were not just groups of people who spoke the same language. Oh no. They were a temporal representation of their trans-temporal "culture".

Vague concepts are the mind's hired help. They make thinking on your own first unnecessary, and then, if they continue to be employed, impossible. How did we think and speak in the days before there were any cultures? In the Christian West the concept of culture was unneeded, because the Christian doctrine of providence did its work for it, and did it better. Christians understood history not as the rise and fall of cultures, nor as the strife of one culture against another, but as the working out of God's eternal purposes in time. And the whole world, not just this or that individual or nation, was God's field of action. The false and foolish doctrine of Multi-culturalism is thus what has arisen to replace the doctrine of the "one holy, catholic and apostolic Church". It exists to prevent us from acknowledging, and in most cases even from recognizing, that the destiny of that Church is one with the destiny of mankind.

Second, even if we think that "cultures" are something different or more important than I give them credit for, Christianity is not one of them. Christianity is not identifiable with any national church or even a transnational one. Christianity is better described as a divinely authored story, a story more ancient and fundamental even than the Christian Church. The birth of Christ, which we celebrated three weeks ago, was the incarnation of God's eternal Word. And even its incarnation in history *preceded* institutional Christianity. Jesus Christ's arrival on earth was heralded by angels with glad tidings of great Joy to **All People**. As Simeon said, in his prophetic moment, holding the infant Jesus, He is the "glory" of Israel, but the "light" of the world:

> Lord now lettest thou thy servant depart in peace, according to thy word. For
> mine eyes have seen thy salvation, which thou hast prepared before the face

of *all people*, to be a light to lighten the *gentiles* and to be the Glory of thy people *Israel* (Luke, 2:29-32).

Third, and finally, the things that we call cultures, even if you think they have some significance, are no barrier to Christianity. It has been estimated that there are 50,000 converts to Christianity every day in Communist China. Professor David Jeffrey, of Baylor University, and a distinguished auxiliary professor of Peking University, has said that in his opinion it is not unthinkable that a new Constantine may arise in China. African Anglicans, as many of you will know, not only outnumber the Anglicans in the rest of the world but are the main pillars of orthodoxy in the Anglican Church. And South American Christians are rekindling both Roman Catholic and Protestant religious zeal.

Multiculturalism, then, is a vague and dubious concept; it does not apply to Christianity, which is a divinely written story and, to the extent that culture is anything, it is no barrier to the universality of the Christian message.

Now some Christians who uncritically admit the concept of multiculturalism into their minds are led by it to make false judgements about evangelization, which limit their effectiveness. Many think that one needs to learn a great deal about other religions before one can begin to evangelize among their believers. And since it takes forever to learn anything useful about another religion, and since legions of them are represented in most public situations, little evangelization gets done. It is important to see the fallacy involved in the idea that evangelization requires study of other religions. No doubt whatever you happen to know about another religion may come in handy in talking with those who believe it, but special knowledge is quite unnecessary. That is because the Gospel message is not directed at ideas, but at the ordinary human situation. And the genius of Opus Dei lies to a great extent in the recognition of this fact. The gospel says that Jesus Christ can free men and women from their burdens and that he is the embodiment of all their hopes. It is not a comparative message but a simple declaration. If the people we live and work with have any burdens or hopes (and could they really be people, if they had not?) then that declaration should interest them. Our job is simply to proclaim it in word and deed. The rest is not our business. The part of the Holy Ghost is to open their eyes.

Speaking of eyes suggests a homely metaphor. Religious convictions are like eyeglasses, they enable us to focus on things that we otherwise would not be able to see clearly. To be a Christian, for instance, is to be able to see humility, piety, wealth, sexuality, power and many other aspects of life in ways to which non-Christians are often completely or at least partially blind. The Opus Dei idea of the witness of work is very important here. Just as sighted people inevitably become leaders when working with the blind, so serious Christians will become leaders when working with those whose religion or lack of religion makes them unable to see clearly. We do not need to try to understand their religion, but only to *practice* our own. Let them judge whether our Christian practices are any truer to life than their own. If they are not, we should expect no converts. Saint Josemaria puts it this way in *Conversations*:

> In fact there are many separated brethren who feel attracted by the spirit of Opus Dei and who cooperate in our apostolate, and they include ministers, even bishops of their respective confessions. As contacts increase, we receive more and more proofs of affection and cordial understanding. And it is because the members of Opus Dei centre their spirituality simply on trying to live responsibly the commitments and demands of Christian Baptism. ... Here they find, put into living practice, a good many of the doctrinal presuppositions in which they, and we Catholics, have placed so many well-founded ecumenical expectations.

Intra-mural Evangelization

That fine passage also puts its delicate finger on my second hot potato: What about Christians evangelizing other Christians? intra-mural evangelization I might call it. Should Roman Catholics be evangelizing Orthodox and Protestant Christians? And what about the other way around? I wish to say that a certain amount of discerning evangelism is good in both directions.

The blessing of the Roman Catholic Church during the whole tenure of its present Pope has been so obvious that many Protestants have gladly acknowledged the spiritual leadership of Rome at this time. The Roman Catholic Church has led us to a more perfect recognition of God's intention for women in the Church and for homosexuals. It has brought us to a more Christian understanding of birth control, abortion, euthanasia, and other social issues to such an extent that it is impossible not to feel attracted to it and annoyed by the seeming rudderlessness of those "ecclesial communities" which lack a Magisterium.

Yet a prominent Roman Catholic speaker addressing a group of fervent Protestant believers brought out another important point. "I have more in common with you guys," he said, "than with those inside my own church who do not take their faith seriously." I doubt that there are many serious Christians here who have not recognized this fact, even if they have never had the occasion to say it in public.

Moreover, at least since Vatican II, Roman Catholics have been prepared to acknowledge that Protestantism has made, and, many would say, continues to make valuable contributions to the Christian family. Never has this been shown more generously than in a pre-Vatican II book by the French Jesuit priest Louis Bouyer, called *The Spirit and Forms of Protestantism*, recently reissued by Sceptre books. Bouyer acknowledges the ongoing contribution of Protestant piety, while arguing that it can only find its fulfillment within the greater Roman Catholic Church.

As one born a Protestant, and open to, but not yet called to Roman Catholicism, I find Bouyer's argument deeply persuasive, and even inevitable. Like Bouyer and the Holy Father, I think it possible and delightful to look forward to a day when we will all be one. Like them again, I find it unthinkable that unity can come about in any other way than by those who once left in protest rejoining the mother Church. But under the leadership of the present Pope, we have all come to see that we need not and should not rush toward such a union. The error of the kind of ecumenism sought by the World Council of Churches is that it is willing to compromise to get there quickly. But *no* truth available to the Church should be allowed to perish in the process of union, including whatever lights the Protestants have managed to keep alive—lights of liturgy, lights of community, lights of preaching, lights of piety, lights of biblical literacy, lights of closeness to Christ. These are not inconsiderable lights, and it would be wrong to hide them under a bushel.

Thus it seems to me also—though this is perhaps not the best locale in which to advertise the opinion—that intramural evangelization ought still to be able to go in both directions. There seem to me to be Roman Catholics—I know some, particularly from Quebec—who are so burned by their bad experiences in the Roman Catholic Church that they are unlikely to return to it, though one can never discount the power of the grace of God. For some of them, at least, Protestant churches will be a necessary stepping stone on their way back to faith, and for more than a few Protestantism may be their lifelong home.

It has been my own experience to have joyful contact with members of Opus Dei communities to whose houses I have been invited as a speaker and of whose gentle attempts to nudge me toward a more Roman faith I have been gratefully aware. But I have found them also to be, as their founder says they should be, respectfully willing to work together in common enterprises for good. There is a great harvest to be reaped and the workers are few. Our common faith and hope encourage us to believe that those who work together in charity will not be found wantingwhen the harvest Master calls us to account.

CARLOS CAVALLÉ

OPUS DEI AND THE WORKS OF MERCY,
AN INTRODUCTION

My task is to introduce the topic of Opus Dei and the Works of Mercy. The next two speakers will deal with specific cases.

Anyone who looks into Christianity will find it said repeatedly that Christians are followers of Christ. Christianity is not an ideology. Being a Christian does not mean belonging to an organization. No. Being a Christian means being a follower of Christ. If we miss this one point, we miss everything.

Now if we want to be followers of Christ, we have to get to know him through the Gospels, where we find his works, his deeds, and his words. Everything we can find out about him, we find in the Gospels. And in the Gospels, we see that Jesus Christ is very close to the poor, very close to the underprivileged, very close to marginal people like people with leprosy, very close to people who suffer. And Christians have practiced works of mercy from the very beginning. From the *Acts of the Apostles* to Mother Teresa of Calcutta one can see a sequence of works of mercy that have been undertaken within Christianity. These works are a manifestation of the love of men and women for God, and through God, for their neighbors. These works are nothing but a way of concretizing what Jesus said: "What you do for these little ones, you do for me."

Even before Opus Dei was founded in 1928, Josemaria Escriva, then a young priest, acting as a responsible Christian, practiced works of mercy. St. Josemaria spent much time with the poor, with the sick, with the less privileged, with Gypsies and other groups who were marginal at that time. He was involved with them to such an extent and with such intensity, dedication, and generosity, that later on he would say that Opus Dei was born among the poor and the sick in the slums and hospitals of Madrid. And even some of the first vocations to Opus Dei came from these hospitals. I am thinking of Maria Ignacia Escobar, who had an irreversible, terminal disease.

Later on St. Josemaria, speaking about the beginnings of Opus Dei, would say, "Do you know where I get this strength, this fortitude? I got them from the sick, from the poor, from the marginal people in my early years in Madrid." And when Opus Dei started its formational activities for the first time, with a small number of university students, a custom was immediately established— Our Lady's visits to the poor. These young university students, after taking part in a formational activity on Saturday, would collect a small amount of money and visit the poor and people who were alone, just to give them their love, their warmth, and also some treats, of course. This has become a custom in Opus Dei, and a tradition that has been maintained along the seventy-five years since its foundation.

Opus Dei, as it developed by the grace of God, has practiced works of mercy of all kinds though its members and cooperators, working individually or together. There are so many interesting initiatives that I am not going to enumerate them. But all of these initiatives are related to specific needs that are found in the places where Opus Dei members and cooperators live. Many of these works of mercy have to do with education for people of all ages, for children, for parents of lesser economic means or social standing. Others have to do with health care: hospitals, for example. Other initiatives are related to sports: sports centers, recreational activities. But whatever these initiatives are, they are always accompanied by Christian formation adapted to the age, the characteristics, and the circumstances of the people attending. For a human being is a unity of soul and body, and both aspects have to be taken into account by Christians and deserve their attention.

So the poor, the underprivileged, the drug addicts, the disabled, the homeless, the ignorant, immigrants, have been the object of works of mercy of Opus Dei members and cooperators. But not only those groups. As John Paul II states very clearly in *The Church in America*, we should exercise a preferential option for the poor, but not an exclusive preference. Pope John Paul refers to other groups in society that are very poor in some ways and deserve special attention, the same attention we should give to those who are poor in economic terms. He talks about politicians, businessmen, medical doctors, and other people who are in some ways privileged people in society. Yet they are also not so privileged, because they lack something that is needed both for their spiritual development and for the development of their social responsibilities. This is why Opus Dei has developed initiatives addressed to these people, including, as I say, businessmen, medical doctors, and other professionals in Europe and North America, as well as in Asia, Central America, and Africa, the neglected-continent. How much work still has to be done in Africa! But in Africa you can find business schools promoted by Opus Dei members and cooperators. You can see racially integrated colleges like Strathmore, hospitals, and centers for the education of women, for mothers of families.

The works of mercy that have been developed around the world during the seventy-five years of the existence of Opus Dei are very impressive. I am not going to give statistics, because the works of mercy are not a matter of statistics, but a matter of true concern for the needy, true fraternity with the needy, true solidarity with the needy, that comes from loving Christ, and through him loving our neighbors. Christ himself said it to us: "Love one another as I have loved you. In this they will recognize that you are my disciples." And there should be no discrimination in our love. Works of mercy will always be needed because, as Jesus Christ said, the poor will always be with us. The poor and the less privileged are a way Christ has of showing his presence in the world. We should see Jesus Christ in these less privileged people, in these poor people, as was mentioned this morning when we were talking about Mother Teresa and love of the sick. Therefore, where there is a Christian, there should always be works of mercy. And this is the case with those who have received the vocation to Opus Dei. In their many initiatives to help the less privileged, members and cooperators of Opus Dei are following the example of St. Josemaria, the founder, whom some of us call our father. And he in turn was following the example given by Jesus Christ when he lived among us.

Audience, St. Michael's College, University of Toronto, January 11, 2003

M. SHARON HEFFERAN

SAINT JOSEMARIA ESCRIVA:
AN INSPIRATION FOR WORKS OF MERCY

In Chicago, forty-three percent of high school students drop-out before graduation. As a response to this astounding statistic, there are over 300 after-school academic programs in the city. The Metro Achievement Center and its brother program, the Midtown Center, serve approximately 1000 inner-city children each year. The centers offer academic enrichment, a character education program based on virtues, and individual mentoring to African-American and Hispanic children between the ages of 9 and 17 who come from impoverished urban Chicago neighborhoods. Over the past three years, 95% of our graduating students have not only finished high school, but have continued on to college.

What makes Metro stand out among hundreds of after-school programs in Chicago? I believe that foremost among the defining characteristics is St. Josemaria Escriva's vision regarding the dignity of the human person, his holistic approach to personal and educational development, and his challenge to the laity to take a significant and personal role in carrying out works of mercy. In this presentation I will focus on the features of our program that embody Escrivá's vision.

On a personal note, I was delighted that the organizing committee of this conference suggested "Works of Mercy" as the context for our presentation on social programs. Often educational programs such as Metro are considered in relation to social justice, but I think that "works of mercy" more accurately describes our work and captures the teachings of St. Josemaría because it points to the heart and soul of our efforts with inner city children. Mercy goes beyond justice. Mercy encourages us to serve and to meet the needs of others out of love, not just strict duty. Works of mercy include the dimension of divine pity, namely a concern for the poor and underprivileged which is at the same time both human and spiritual.[1]

The fifth beatitude reminds us: "Blessed are the merciful, for they shall see God." Seeing one race, the race of the children of God, is a major tenet of Escriva's writings. I would add that treating each individual girl as a child of God is the context for all of our educational work at Metro.

---

[1] Gerald Vann, *The Divine Pity: A Study in the Social Implications of the Beatitudes*, Fount Paperbacks, 1985, p. 120.

In this paper I would like to focus on three ideas derived from St. Josemaría's thought that directly influence our work with economically disadvantaged children: Unity of the Human and Divine or "Unity of Life"; Fostering Faith in a Secular Setting; and Primacy of Individuals over Institutions and Structures

Unity of the human and divine

Escriva often spoke of "unity of life" —the harmony between the different facets of a person's life— namely, that the human and divine dimensions of our existence are distinct but intertwined and inseparable. The unity between the human and divine is reinforced in several ways at Metro.

Students are encouraged to work well, not just for themselves, but with an eye to serving others and the common good. Escriva's teaching that work can be a prayer offered to God is often a new discovery for both students and volunteers.

We make a concerted effort to keep the facility clean, orderly, and non-institutional in appearance, thus living out what St. Josemaría referred to as "Christian materialism". We strive to reflect this in the attractive décor and cleanliness of the center itself.

For a social program to be a work of mercy, a Christian spirit is essential to its being. I was reminded of this several years ago by a woman with whom I was speaking about my trips to Lithuania to lead the English Camps organized by Opus Dei. After explaining to her that we offered classes in English, character education, and sports, I mentioned that we also offered religious education. This woman's response was pointed and clear: "I'm sure glad to hear that you include the option of attending religious education classes because Opus Dei isn't here to do social work. There are plenty of wonderful agencies providing social services. If Opus Dei isn't here to help people get closer to God, why bother?" This story brings to mind those words of St. Josemaría which often serve as a reminder to those of us who strive to help the needy: "Until now you had not understood the message that we Christians bring to the rest of men: the hidden marvel of the interior life. What a wonderful new world you are placing in front of them!"[2]

Part of the effort to "materialize" the faith and facilitate that connection between faith and life is placing a chapel right in the middle of our academic space. The staff, students and volunteers can stop in at any time to pray. We do not have any mandatory religious services as part of the program, yet the chapel serves as a physical reminder of how natural our relationship with God should be in the midst of the simple and ordinary things in life: our learning, socializing, volunteer and service work.

Our holistic approach to education —educating the mind, heart, body, and soul— emphasizes that link between the human and divine in each person and brings about remarkable growth in the girls we serve. It is Escriva's keen

---

[2]*Furrow*, 654.

appreciation for the unity that should exist within the person (and should be therefore reflected in the education of each child) that influences the academic program and curricula in our centers.

Fostering Faith in a Secular Setting

The work done at Metro is directed and carried out by lay persons, and it is not an ecclesial work. St. Josemaría challenged lay people to feel personally responsible for discovering solutions to society's problems; raising up the poor is not a task meant to be left for clerics and religious to solve. Concretely, Metro and Midtown work with approximately 500 professional volunteers from the city of Chicago who are encouraged to engage their hands and hearts by serving inner-city children. We operate with funds received neither from the Church nor from Opus Dei but rather from corporations and foundations that contribute 80% of our income.

Our academic and character programs are offered to all students. Students interested in learning more about the Catholic faith need to "opt-in" to religion classes with parental permission. At Metro you will find a natural and positive approach to faith, a respect for all faiths, and an opportunity to explore the Catholic faith, if interested.

In this way, Metro is a fabulous meeting ground and environment where students and volunteers of all faiths can grow both humanly and spiritually. When a professional woman or college student comes to tutor and help a child academically, they often discover in the process something deeper; friendship and love of God. At Metro we prefer to speak of "self-worth" rather than self-esteem precisely because true self-esteem springs naturally from a girl's aware-ness of her personal dignity and her value in God's eyes. It is precisely in this pro-faith environment in the center that students, their families, and volunteers often discover —or rediscover— the faith that they may have abandoned years ago. It is precisely in our secular setting that laity have the unique opportunity to bring the faith beyond the walls of the parish church and faith community.

Priority of the Individual over the Institution

In Chapter 5 of the Gospel of St. Luke we read about the parables of God's mercy: the lost sheep that God seeks out among the other 100; the joy of God over one sinner who repents; the Father's desire to forgive and welcome back the prodigal son. In all of these parables we are reminded of the value of the individual, of the importance of each person who is loved and sought out by God's mercy.

Our modern age is one of elaborate structures and institutions. Financial and commercial institutions influence and regulate our monetary well-being. Global networks of communication and technology have institutionalized and revolutionized the way we work and communicate. Even in the Church, in recent decades, religious institutions have developed and served the needs of the poor by establishing global structures. Metro itself is a large institution that serves the needs of the Chicago poor through its after-school and summer programs. However, St. Josemaria would warn us against developing an institutional or collective mentality towards helping the less fortunate. He reminded us that God cures and reaches out to souls one-by-one and that we too are most effective when our works of charity reach the individual person. We must therefore take care not to get lost in building programs or institutions if this endeavor leads us to lose sight of the individual people we are serving.

A few months ago a young woman came to Metro looking for a job. When we spoke about the needs of inner city children, she appealed to the reformation of structures as the answer to their plight. She commented, "If we could just reform the structures in the Chicago school system we'd have justice for the poor." I appreciated her youthful insistence but I challenged her. I told her that our educational philosophy at Metro is to focus on the *person* rather than the structure. I agreed with her assertion that just structures and institutions certainly facilitate justice. However, I argued that structures themselves are not the ultimate cause of injustice, nor are they the solution. St. Josemaria (and John Paul II) would argue that the answer to injustice lies with *individuals* who act justly. If individuals are just, over time the structures and institutions that employ them will be just.[3] Taking this line of reasoning one step further, one must serve not only with justice but also with charity. In the words of Escrivá, "justice alone is never enough to solve the great problems of mankind... The dignity of man, who is a son of God, requires much more. Charity must penetrate and accompany justice, because it sweetens and deifies everything: 'God is love'."[4]

It is this personalistic approach, this focus on the individual, the concern for their spiritual well-being and eternal happiness, as well as their physical and academic progress, that helps the children we work with blossom into the strong and caring adults they were created to be.

Precisely because of our conviction that people, not structures, are what really count, each girl in our program receives individual attention either from a tutor or a mentor, or both. At any given time, approximately 200 professional and university women work with 300 young girls to make this personal attention a mainstay of our program. I firmly believe that individual attention and our faith-inclusive approach to education is what brings about such far-reaching and positive results in the lives of the people we serve.

Conclusion

To conclude, I would like to emphasize that St. Josemaria's love for each human person as a child of God who needs to be nurtured and loved for who they are is the vision that shapes the work that we do in the inner city of

---

[3] José-Luis Illanes, "Work, Justice, Charity," *Holiness and the World*, Scepter, Princeton, N.J., 1997, 226-227.

[4] *Friends of God*, Scepter, 172.

Chicago. Escriva's belief that a deep furrow of true human development can only take place when there is an appreciation of both the human and the divine, gives our work of mercy the impetus and strength to build up the inner city poor from within. The hidden work of education is always effective when we treat others as children of God. Of that St. Josemaría was convinced. I quote from his writings: "A son of God cannot entertain class prejudice, for he is interested in the problems of all men. And he tries to help solve them with the justice and charity of our Redeemer."[5]

---

[5]*Furrow*, 303..

ANTHONY YEOW

THE ACADEMIC AND SPORTS ENRICHMENT PROGRAM

In 1994, a group of university students from Ernescliff College launched the Academic and Sports Enrichment Program (ASE), a program for inner city boys in Toronto. We were inspired to take this action by the teaching of St. Josemaria Escriva. In July 2000, an umbrella charitable organization was formed, called Toronto Youth Development, which funds ASE and, we hope, will fund a similar program for girls in the future.

Let me begin by telling you two personal encounters I've had with two Regent Park children who have been in our programs, one in Grade 6 and the other in Grade 8. These two encounters are deeply engraved in my mind because they awakened my heart and helped me to understand more deeply the meaning of sanctification of work. The first conversation involved a child whose family has been living in Regent Park for three generations. I asked him a question that we, as adults, like to ask a child: "When you're grown up, what would you like to be?" He responded, "What do you mean by that?" "You know what I mean," I said. "Perhaps you want to be a doctor, a banker, a scientist, some kind of work that you think you would like to do in the future, so that you can raise a family." He answered, "Is it necessary to work? I have not seen anyone in my family work before. Mom is always home and we still have a house to live in, food to eat, and clothes to wear. Work is boring and tiring, just like homework. I think it's more fun to play basketball than to work."

On another occasion, I was talking to a boy, recently immigrated from India. I asked a similar question: "Have you been studying hard, like your mother said?" He replied, "Yup, I have to study hard, get a good job and make a tonne of money." "What do you want to do with all this money?" I asked. He said, "Buy a big house and a Ferrari. I want a lot of money so that I can buy many things for myself and my family, and life will be very happy for all of us."

What a contrast! Even at a very young age, children can form very different attitudes toward the meaning of work. One perceives work as almost a punishment and the other as a means to achieve material comfort. How can we respond to both of them? St. Josemaria gives us the answer very simply and eloquently. In a homily he gave on the feast of St. Joseph in 1963, he said, "Work, all work, bears witness to the dignity of man, to his dominion over creation. It is an opportunity to develop one's personality. It is a bond of union with others, the way to support one's family, a means of helping to improve the society in which we live and the progress of all humanity."[1] Work is a means of helping to improve the society in which we live and the progress of all humanity! How many of us actually think work can have such a macro impact? Yet St. Josemaria passionately and insistently preached to the world that work is a means and path to holiness; it is something to be sanctified and something which sanctifies others.

A profound understanding of the real meaning of work will position us to acquire the real meaning of works of mercy. According to the *Catechism of the Catholic Church*, "The Works of Mercy are charitable actions by which we come to the aid of our neighbour in his spiritual and bodily necessities. Instructing, advising, consoling are spiritual works of mercy, as are forgiving and bearing wrongs patiently" (#2447). The Church has always encouraged the faithful to engage in works of mercy. It is to be hoped that through justice and our charity, we may alleviate another person's suffering. More importantly, we can help them to sanctify their condition. A work of mercy can do an immense amount of good for the people who are suffering as well as for the people who stretch out their hands to help.

One of the hardest places to try to do it well is the inner city. Just east of Toronto's Eaton Centre, the Regent Park area (the oldest and largest public housing project in Canada) exemplifies the inner city's reality. Here childhood is brief. The family, often headed by a single mother, struggles to make ends meet. Drugs and gang violence lure children away from their fragile home lives and into a seemingly never-ending cycle of despair.

Where these children end up is no great surprise: in dead end, low paying jobs, at best. Many join the millions of unemployed, disillusioned young people on the street and in gangs. The basic lessons of what is right and what is wrong often take a back seat to daily survival. The cost of the drop-out rate, along with the pervasive presence of drugs and crime, is enormous and has to be measured in far more than economic or monetary terms. Entire neighbourhoods, whole families and countless individuals are hurt by this failure.

You will be appalled by the statistics I give you. They paint a grim picture. Demographic indicators provided by the City of Toronto show that 55.7% of Regent Park's families are single parent families. Youth unemployment stands at 32.9%, which is more than double the city's rate of 16%. The number of youth who do not finish Grade 9 is also twice the city's average, and only 6.2% of them make it to university, while university attendance in the rest of the city is at 25.7%.

People in Toronto expect only bad news from Regent Park. It is one of those inner city communities condemned in the mind of the public to failure — and certainly to a bad press. Most people only hear about the negative aspects of Regent Park. You do not hear about young people who achieve a lot because that is not news. This bad image needs to be changed.

---

[1] *Christ is Passing By*, 47.

We launched ASE in the hope of alleviating this situation. We hoped to motivate the children of Regent Park in their studies and to help them discover the value and meaning of learning and work. We realised that to break the cycle of despair, we had to penetrate one generation, and it was clear to us that we'd have to start with children.

We also discovered that there are many existing programs in Regent Park. But they deal mainly with the symptoms of a deeper problem. They try to keep these children out of drugs and gangs by keeping them busy with many sporting activities. But the real solution is to build inner-directed and habitual strengths of mind and will within them. In short, to foster true character, and to help them acquire virtues like responsibility, honesty, respect for self and others, spirit of service, and living out duties to family and community.

ASE runs a summer enrichment program, led by university and college students who dedicate six weeks of summer holidays to Regent Park youth, giving them a fun-filled and fulfilling summer, as well as a head-start for the new school year. Students take math and English in the morning and participate in competitive sports in the afternoon. The academic courses emphasize and reinforce fundamentals. More importantly, the curriculum is geared to help them discover that learning can be fun and yet challenging.

Character development is an important component; students attend a character class each day. Drills and training form an integral part of the afternoon sports period, emphasizing the importance of teamwork, practice and achievement. Students are divided into groups and participate in competitive sports based on a tournament schedule. Excursions, educational field trips and outdoor camping are organized to complement the summer fun that every child wants.

Throughout the year, career talks are arranged to help the students explore different career opportunities. Community service projects (such as community garden cleaning and visits to old age homes) are scheduled to instil civic and social responsibility.

Discipline often poses a special problem for the counsellors. As Dean of Character Education in Northmount School, I often hear from parents that they have a very hard time disciplining their children at home; they find them very demanding. But I tell them that teachers have unique problems that parents don't have. No parent, as far as I know, has to discipline 20 children at home.

Talking about discipline, I have to share with you one of the ASE stories. About four years ago, we brought 40 boys from the ASE programs to the Ontario Science Centre. We divided ourselves into five different groups with a university student counsellor leading each group, and happily entered the Science Centre. I was the Program Director that year, so I took a walk around just to make sure that everything was going well. Within half an hour, I heard the fire alarm go off. Then I heard the over the P.A. system, "The person in charge of the ASE group, please go to the security desk." I proceeded to the security and was informed that two of our children had pulled the alarm. I apologized and took the two boys out. As we were walking out, one counsellor came running to me and told me that he had caught four boys stealing ice cream from the cafeteria. So we went to get those boys and I was going to call it a day for the field trip. When we reached the foyer of the main entrance, the employee at the coffee counter told me that one of our boys had taken the penny jar and run away.

This field trip was a real disaster. At that moment, all the counsellors and myself were frustrated, furious, and at the same time exhausted. The only thing that could come to mind now was to pray. I said, "God, God, what's wrong with these kids? Guardian angels come to our rescue." You can imagine the anxiety we were going through, but unexpectedly we managed to remain calm and solve all the problems we had—one at a time. Somehow, I understood the meaning of turning work into prayer. St Josemaria once said, "We see the hand of God not only in wonders, but also in an experience of work and effort. Work thus becomes prayer and thanksgiving, because we know we are placed on earth by God...in all that you do, do everything for God's glory (1 Cor 10:31)."[2] He went on to say, "When you feel your weakness, the failures which arise even in human undertakings, you will gain in objectivity, in humility, and in understanding for others. Successes and joys will prompt you to thanksgiving and to realize that you do not live for yourself but for the service of others and of God."[3]

But we do have successes, and they are a great reward. I recently met a former ASE student and he joyfully informed me that he is applying to the University of Toronto and Ryerson University for admission to a Computer Engineering Program. You can imagine my feelings and the feelings of the counsellors who have worked with him.

Toronto Youth Development is a work of mercy inspired by the founder of Opus Dei, St. Josemaria. This work of mercy does not benefit solely the children in Regent Park. It also has a profound and lasting impact on their parents, the counsellors working in the program, and the donors and sponsors of the program. All these people interact with the children in the program. They see that being a role model is not enough. The children need to see that their parents and adults are working too. What will have a lasting impact on them is not the role we play for them but the person we are for them. One person put it eloquently, "This (character education) is really about us, isn't it ... about the way we lead our lives?"

Perseverance is important. Indeed, a work of mercy can be exhausting, discouraging, and at times disappointing. But we must persevere because there is this wonderful gift that God has placed in each of our hearts, your heart and my heart. And that gift is LOVE. Pope John Paul II, in his Apostolic Letter, *Salvifici Doloris*, wrote:

> We could say that suffering, which is present under so many different forms in our human world, is also present in order to unleash love in the human per-

---

[2] *Christ is Passing By,* 48.

[3] *Christ is Passing By,* 49.

son, that unselfish gift of one's 'I' on behalf of other people, especially those who suffer. The world of human suffering, unceasingly calls for, so to speak, another world; the world of human love; and in a certain sense man owes to suffering that unselfish love which stirs in his heart and actions.[4]

This is clearly affirmed and reflected in St. Josemaria's teaching and writing. In *The Way of the Cross*, he wrote: "No matter how much you may love, you will never love enough. The human heart is endowed with an enormous coefficient of expansion. When it loves, it opens out in a crescendo of affection that overcomes all barriers. If you love Our Lord, there will not be a single creature that does not find a place in your heart."

I would like to leave you with this thought of St. Josemaria: Because the world is something good, we should love it passionately.

---

[4] *Salvifici Doloris*, 29.

TERESA A. TOMORY

EDUCATION AND FAMILY: INSIGHTS AND APPLICATION

Introduction

In September 1989, a small group of parents started Hawthorn School for Girls, an independent girls' school, with twenty-two students in five elementary grades in a rented facility in the Beaches area of Toronto. What can be written about the school's history to explain why it exists? How did the school come to be? In order to answer these questions, let us take a step back to examine a bigger picture, the context that better explains the reasons for the school's existence.

For this purpose, I would like to consider the technical and visual elements of a large, beautiful tapestry as a comparison. A tapestry is composed of a warp and a weft.

> The warp, which is nothing but a skeleton structure, disappears completely beneath the body of the fabric. All that can be seen in a finished tapestry is the weft, made up of different coloured threads forming the decorative scheme. However, the weft threads are not taken systematically right across the width of the warp…but only across that part of the warp corresponding to the coloured area indicated in the section of the cartoon being woven.[1]

> The subject matter or theme of a tapestry is visually presented through the many scenes constructed by the multitude of interwoven threads of the weft. These threads of many colours and hues are woven through the warp until it is entirely encased in the finished tapestry. However the warp, though invisible, provides the foundational structure for the whole work. All the individual threads of the weft are an integral part of the design. No pattern or image would be visible without these threads.

I will speak about the story of Hawthorn School for Girls in terms of a warp, an underlying foundation, and the many threads of the weft, which create the scenes and patterns of the full composition. The warp of the tapestry is provided by the universal call to holiness and to apostolate, which are consequences of baptism. The threads of the weft are provided by our vocations as married people and parents living in ordinary circumstances in the middle of the world, and by the specific needs that led to the creation of Hawthorn

---

[1] *Great Tapestries*, edited by Joseph Jobe, Edita S.A.Lausanne, 1965, p. 227.

School. The tapestry can be entitled *The Grandeur of Ordinary Life*, with the story of Hawthorn School comprising a small part of this vast picture. Most of you will recognize the title, *The Grandeur of Ordinary Life,* as the theme of a conference, which took place in Rome in January 2002, to commemorate the centennial of the birth of the St. Josemaria. Since today's event also honours him, the title for the tapestry seemed appropriate.

Sanctity and Apostolate

For many of us Hawthorn School is a dream, which has become a reality. This phenomenon has been repeated many times in different places with different individuals over the course of the last 75 years since that day of October 2,1928, when St. Josemaria "saw" Opus Dei. This dream of Hawthorn really started with the St. Josemaria who envisioned a multitude of Christian men and women present at all levels of society who would "light up the paths of the earth with faith and love"[2] by their prayer and actions, freely assuming their responsibilities as children of God. St. Josemaria described his dream in a homily:

> I dream—and the dream has come true —of multitudes of God's children, sanctifying themselves as ordinary citizens, sharing the ambitions and endeavours of their colleagues and friends. . . . He has invited you to stay among the activities and concerns of the world .He wants you to know that your human vocation, your profession, your talents are not omitted from his divine plan. . . The commandment God gives us is to love as he has loved us, which in most cases means living alongside of others and being their equals, giving ourselves to the service of our Lord in the world so as to make every-one know better the love of God, telling them that the divine paths of the world have been opened up.[3]

Sanctity and apostolate form part of the warp, the underlying structure of our tapestry. Men and women have taken to heart this call to be holy and to be apostles in the middle of the world, desiring to make this a reality in themselves and in those around them through all the possibilities offered by the temporal world. Saint Josemaria emphasized many times that this striving for sanctity and apostolate is the task of the ordinary Christian: "Opus Dei proposes to help the ordinary citizen like yourself to lead a fully Christian life, without modify-ing their normal way of life, their daily work, their aspirations and ambitions. Opus Dei aims to encourage people in every sector of society to desire holiness in the midst of the world."[4]

You and I are "the ordinary citizen." We live in all layers of society, in ordinary circumstances of daily life, sharing all the social conditions, concerns, and cares of our fellow citizens of the world around us. Through our baptism

---

[2]From the "prayer card" distributed by the Opus Dei Prelature..

[3]*Christ is Passing By,* 20-21.

[4]*Conversations with Msgr. Escriva,* 24.

we are able to identify ourselves with Christ and lead others to Christ. We want to take our sanctification seriously and seek to help others to do the same.

The grace of the sacrament of baptism constitutes another essential component of the warp of our tapestry. At the beatification of the St. Josemaria on May 17,1992 Pope John Paul II stated in his homily:

> Indeed in Baptism by which we become God's children we receive grace, that seed of holiness that grows and matures with the help of the other sacraments and the practice of piety. This is what the same Blessed reminds us.... Christians working in the midst of the world, must reconcile all things with God, speaking with Christ in the midst of all human activity. Particularly in our day Christians are called to co-operate in a new evangelization that imbues the home, professional life, centres of culture and work, mass media, public and private life with those Gospel values that are the source of peace, beauty, ...This call was repeatedly promoted by St. Josemaria.[5]

Each of us, as lay persons living in the middle of the world, find ourselves in a specific place that contains many opportunities for growth in holiness and for apostolate. The way in which many people seize these opportunities provides threads for the weft of the tapestry. In another interview recorded in *Conversations,* St. Josemaria said,

> Lay people have their own way of contributing to the holiness and apostolate of the Church. They do so by their free and responsible action within the temporal sphere, to which they bring the leaven of Christianity. Giving Christian witness in their everyday lives, spreading the word which enlightens in the name of God, acting responsibly in the service of others and thus contributing to the solution of common problems; these are some of the ways in which ordinary Christians fulfil their divine mission.[6]

St. Josemaria taught that we should assume the responsibilities of our particular circumstances always acting in full freedom in regard to temporal realities, "to fulfil the mission which God has given you, in the place and in the environment indicated by his Providence."[7]

Family and Education

In the context of this presentation, the specific locus of our activity is family and education, which provide more threads for our tapestry. For most of us our vocation and mission will be found in married and family life. This is the particular place where we will seek God's will for us. Over the years St. Josemaria spoke many times about the importance and dignity of marriage and family life, emphasizing that "marriage is a divine path on earth to lead those with

---

[5]Pope John Paul II, Homily, May 17, 1992.

[6]*Conversations* , #59.

[7]*Conversations*, # 60.

whom we live to God."[8] In a homily, *Marriage, a Christian Vocation,* he said,

> Husband and wife are called to sanctify their married life and to sanctify themselves in it. It would be a serious mistake if they were to exclude family life from their spiritual development. The marriage union, the care and education of children, the effort to provide for the needs of the family as well as for its security and development, the relationship with other persons who make up the community, all these are among the ordinary human situations that Christian couples are called upon to sanctify.[9]

He called families "the cells of Christianity" affirming that "the first apostolate is in the home ...parents should understand that founding a family, educating their children, and exercising a Christian influence in society, are supernatural tasks."[10] The mission of parents is to provide the environment their children require in order to develop into mature responsible adults. Again in the homily, *Marriage, a Christian Vocation*, St. Josemaria tells us, "Parents are called to cooperate with the Holy Spirit in the development of their children into men and women who will be authentic Christians."[11]

In this sense we describe the role of the parents as primary educators of their children. The parents' task to educate their children stems from natural law and they are enabled to fulfil their responsibilities by the graces received through baptism and marriage. This has been the perennial teaching of the Church. One of the documents of the Second Vatican Council, *Gravissimum Educationis*, states, "Since parents have conferred life on their children, they have a most solemn obligation to educate their offspring. Hence, parents must be acknowledged as the first and foremost educators of their children. Their role as educators is so decisive that scarcely anything can compensate for their failure in it."[12] In his apostolic letter, *Familiaris Consortio*, Pope John Paul II, writes,

> The right and duty of parents to give education is essential, since it is connected with the transmission of human life; it is original and primary with regard to the educational role of others, on account of the uniqueness of the loving relationship between parents and children; it is irreplaceable and inalienable, and therefore incapable of being entirely delegated to others or usurped by others.[13]

The family is the basic cell of society, a microcosm of society. The family as a social unit is also the first educating community of a society where the members of a family are constantly interacting and learning from each other. It

---

[8]*Conversations,* 91.

[9]*Christ is Passing By,* 23.

[10]*Conversaions,* 91.

[11]*Christ is Passing By, 27.*

[12]Vatican Council II,*Grav.Ed., #3.*

[13]Pope John Paul II,*Fam.Cons.#36.*

is uniquely suited to the transmission of ethical, cultural and social values essential to the development and well being of the individual and by extension of society. As such the family should be encouraged and supported to fulfil its functions in order to benefit all of society. Because the state of health of the family is critical for the development and improvement of a nation, the education provided within the family is of the utmost importance.

One of St. Josemaria's major concerns was the preservation, revitalization, and strengthening of the family. He emphasized that the family that reflects the light of Christ will have "a home full of light and cheerfulness" and as such will be the guide of the world"[14] He exhorts families to be "sowers of peace and joy..... ...This is what we have to be."[15] In homilies, writings, and meeting people, he presented many points for parents' reflection in the education of their children in the home. The importance of the parents' example was a primary consideration.

> Parents teach their children mainly through their own conduct. What a son or daughter looks for in a father or mother is not only a certain amount of knowledge . . . [but] a proof of the value and meaning of life, shown through the life of a specific person and confirmed in the different situations and circumstances that occur over a period of time . . . Don't let yourself be deceived: they see everything from their earliest years, and they judge everything. Let them see that God is not only on your lips but also in your deeds.[16]

> Two other important responsibilities for parents to carry out in the home are education in the faith and the introduction to a life of piety. Parents have the mission to educate their children in the faith, guiding them to prayer and the sacraments. St. Josemaria said, "Experience shows in all Christian environments what good effects come from the natural and supernatural introduction to the life of piety given in the warmth of the home...They learn to pray following their parents' example."[17] The life of piety in a child is fostered and developed through the parents' example.

Another feature of St. Josemaria's approach to Christian education is the importance placed upon the human virtues, and their acquisition especially in the home. In a homily in *Friends of God*, he writes, " The human virtues . . . are the foundation for the supernatural ones. These in turn provide us with constant encouragement to behave as good human beings. In either case it is not sufficient merely to want to have these virtues. We have to learn how to practice them."[18] In another homily he points out that the home is the place where children will first learn the practice of the virtues both supernatural faith, hope

[14]*Christ is Passing By, 30.*

[15]*loc. cit.*

[16]*Christ is Passing By, 28.*

[17]*Conversations,* 103.

[18]*Friends of God, 91.*

and charity, and natural virtues, "prudence, loyalty, sincerity, humility, industriousness, cheerfulness. . . ." Thus parents will sanctify their family life thereby creating a true family atmosphere.[19]

As my final point in considering education within the family, St. Josemaria always advised parents to respect their children's legitimate freedom: "Parents have to respect their children's freedom because there is no real education without personal responsibility, and there is no responsibility without freedom."[20] He emphasized the vital importance for parents to develop a relationship of trust and confidence with their children. The relationship between the parent and the child is critical in helping to develop the child's personality and transmitting essential values Many times he gave parents the advice not to behave in a dictatorial manner with their children, stating that "Imposing things by force, in an authoritarian manner, is not the right way to teach. The ideal attitude of parents lies more in becoming their children's friends—friends who will be willing to share their anxieties, who will listen to their problems, who will help them in an effective and agreeable way."[21]

Parents and the School

The next thread we will examine is that of parents and their connection with the school. In *Christ is Passing By,* St. Josemaria said, "The parents are the first persons responsible for the education of their children in human as well as spiritual matters. They should be conscious of the extent of their responsibility."[22] After the family, the next social community whose responsibility includes the development of the child is the school. In most circumstances the family does not undertake to deliver all the components which comprise a complete education. The work done in the home will be supplemented by the work of the school. The parents, as the ones who are first and foremost responsible for their children, seek the help of the school in a complementary role. As the primary educators of their children, it is always incumbent upon them to familiarize themselves with the education that their children receive in the school and to ascertain that this education is consistent with that of the home. This is a right, which may not be taken away from them, and a duty, which they may not give up. Furthermore, the rights and responsibilities of parents both as parents and citizens allow them to start their own schools if it is possible and appropriate.

In 1963, some parents in a get together in Spain with the St. Josemaria were commenting about some worrisome conditions prevalent in the schools at that time. He reassured them that as parents who have received the graces of the sacraments of baptism and matrimony, and as free citizens with a social

---

[18]*Friends of God, 91.*

[19]*Christ is Passing By, 23.*

[20]*Christ is Passing By, 28.*

[21]*Christ is Passing By, 27.*

[22]*loc. cit.*

responsibility, they were able to apply whatever solutions were appropriate to ensure a Christian education for their children. Upon hearing these words of St. Josemaria, these parents took the initiative to found the first of what was to be many schools inspired by his insight. This first school, Gaztelueta, was located in Bilbao, Spain. Soon parents working together with educators started other such schools throughout Spain. Subsequently the model of these schools spread to other countries as parents, becoming more cognizant of their role in the education of their children, rightfully chose this approach to fulfil their responsibilities in this area. These parents had clearly understood their obligation in regard to their children and they recognized their freedom to organize educational centres that supported the work of the parents in the home. These schools work closely with the parents to educate their children and parents continue to exercise the role of primary educator. Today, these schools exist internationally- in the Philippines, in Australia, in the United States, in Europe, in Africa, in the countries of Central and South America, and in Canada, more specifically in Toronto.

Hawthorn School for Girls

The final threads of the tapestry that I will examine describe the scene of Hawthorn School. In its first year Hawthorn had twenty-two students. Today the enrolment is two hundred and twenty in grades ranging from junior kindergarten to grade twelve. The school owns a building of 20,000 square feet and an expansion of 12,000 square feet. is scheduled for completion at the end of the summer. Hawthorn School is a respected member of several professional associations .The annual Gala Dinner raised about $60,000.00 this year. These facts tell you a little bit about the growth of Hawthorn since 1989.The families of the school reflect the diversity of society itself, coming from many different religious, ethnic and socio-economic backgrounds. Hawthorn provides an education based on the teachings of the Catholic Church. Whatever their background, all who share Hawthorn's philosophy and commitment to moral excellence and personal development are welcome at the school.

To get back to the question I raised at the beginning of this presentation, how did Hawthorn School for Girls come to be? I have already described the background and conditions that led to the founding of Hawthorn. Its remote origins can be traced back to a small catechetical initiative that started in 1987. My husband and I invited some families to our home for study sessions for both parents and children to enrich and deepen the knowledge of our faith. The parents gathered together in one room; the children divided into age appropriate groups and went to other areas of the house for their classes. In total there were about 20 children plus their parents. The parents studied the Church documents concerning matters related to the family. The study sessions lasted about 45 minutes and took place during the school year twice a month on a weeknight. By the end of the school year other families had heard about this imitative and also wanted to take part. In September 1988 we were able to continue this

Family Catechism, as it came to be called, in a greatly expanded format. The total number of people, including both parents and children, increased significantly to about 130 people. We were given the use of a very spacious day care centre, which allowed us to accommodate all the groups. The Family Catechism now met on a Saturday morning for two hours. The program expanded from just a study of the catechism to other subjects which included stories about people living both ordinary and heroic virtues, Church history, logic games to help children improve their thinking skills and sports activities. The parents expanded their own program of study in addition to helping in the organization and teaching of the children's classes. The most important criterion for enrolment in the program was the presence and participation of the parent in some way.

Over the course of that year the idea of starting a school was seriously considered. In January 1989, a feasibility study was conducted and a general meeting was held for interested parents. A steering committee was organized to continue the investigation. Based on the findings of the committee, a decision was made in the early spring of 1989 to start a girls' school first, which would be followed by a boys' school at a later date. In June of 1989 we had no teachers, no money, and no location, but we did have twenty-two students. Over the course of that summer the newly constituted Board of Directors was able to find a suitable location, the teachers, and even a school chaplain. The Board of Directors had requested the Prelature of Opus Dei to provide a priest for the spiritual needs of the school. This is how Father Joseph Soria came to be appointed as our first chaplain.

In the first year of the school's existence, long and profound deliberations took place at the level of the Board of Directors as they grappled with the essential elements of the school and how to enunciate and transmit these substantive features to all who would come in contact with the school, especially parents and staff. These elements were eventually published as the *Goals, Principles and Operating Characteristics* of the school. They still serve us well today because they provide a framework, a point of reference for explaining to people, especially to prospective parents and to staff, the fundamental principles of the school. The *Goal* is stated as follows: "To provide children as members of a family unit with an integral education. This education is based upon the natural virtues illuminated by the full recognition of man's supernatural end." The goal recognizes four important things: (1) The child is an inseparable part of a family unit composed of parents and children. (2) The education provided addresses all aspects of formation and development, spiritual, intellectual, human, social, affective, and physical. (3)"The full recognition of man's supernatural end" refers to the fact that each human person is a child of God called to eternal life. Respect for the dignity of the human person, which underlies everything done at the school, is based upon the fact that each person is a child of God. (4) The education in the natural virtues, which constitutes the foundation of the program of character education at Hawthorn School, consists not only of intellectual knowledge of the virtues but also of their integration into daily life.

For the purposes of my presentation here today I will confine myself to highlighting two of the principles:

First, parents are the primary educators of their children; the school founded by parents operates as an aid to parents.

Second, substantial parental involvement is essential and expected. To safeguard and promote the unity of the family and the coherence of the educating endeavour, the school contributes to the formation of the parents and the teachers.

The students are best educated both personally and academically when the school's priorities are ordered first to the parents, then to the faculty, and finally to the students. This is one of the most important features of Hawthorn, indeed, of all the schools inspired by the teachings of St. Josemaria. This hierarchy of parents, teachers, and students is a radical departure from conventional practice. However, this is a fundamental insight of St. Josemaria in regard to schools. Because of the attention that is given to parents to assist them in the education of their children, the school is providing support to the home.

The conscious effort to foster home-school collaboration is done in a variety of ways at Hawthorn. Activities are organized by the school to help parents understand more profoundly their role as primary educators. Guest speakers from various disciplines and areas of expertise are invited to give seminars to the parents. In-house presentations and workshops, such as education in human sexuality, preparing for high school, good study habits, etc., are part of annual parents' programs offered at the different grade levels. Parents have the opportunity to discuss their child's progress with both teachers and advisors Meetings take place at regular intervals in order to set goals for the child in regard to academic issues as well as in those areas which relate to the acquisition of virtues.

The cornerstone of the personal character education at Hawthorn is the advising program, which assists students in the understanding of themselves and their relationship with others. Each student has a faculty advisor with whom she meets regularly throughout the school year. The advisor, by listening, understanding, encouraging, and giving advice, leads the student to discover her strengths and weaknesses and to improve in her academic, personal, and social life .The advisor serves as an essential link between the parents and the school. Through the close contact with parents, advisors support the parental efforts to help their daughters mature.

The faculty, in keeping with these principles, also participates in a program of professional development that helps teachers understand the specific nature of the school. Topics covered in the teachers' program include the school's philosophy of education, understanding the human person and the needs of the human person, current ethical and social issues, integration of the virtues in teaching and curriculum, etc. All of these elements promote a unity between the academic and personal education received in the school and at home as a result of a deliberate and systematic effort to work together. In this way the hierarchy of parents, teachers, and students is developed and maintained. Through these means the school provides valuable support for the family. Family life in the home is strengthened, resulting in strong families. Strong families lead to a healthy society.

Conclusion

We return to our tapestry. We have examined the warp—the structure provided by personal sanctity and apostolate, and the many threads of the weft—vocation and mission in the ordinary circumstances in the midst of the world, social responsibility and freedom to act in regard to temporal realities, the path to sanctity in marriage, the rights and duties of parents, education within the family and parents assuming social responsibilities in regard to education outside the home, and finally Hawthorn School as a specific manifestation of all of the above. All these threads are interwoven to result in the depiction of the *"Grandeur of Ordinary Life"* as taught by Saint Josemaria.

Some day historians will look back and examine the 20th century and recognize two of the most important figures who have had a decisive influence: Pope John Paul II, who exhorts us to re-Christianize society, to re-evangelize the world, to build the civilization of love, and Saint Josemaria, who teaches us how to do it.

DOMINIC MANGANIELLO

THE UNIVERSITY IS FOR DONKEYS

St. Josemaria once described himself as a "university man" with a "passionate interest" in all aspects of higher education.[1] I want to begin by recounting an anecdote that might not at first seem related to my subject but is, in fact, a pre-amble to it. One day a canon at the Cathedral of Valencia asked his good friend Josemaria for a photograph of himself. "Sure," Escriva replied. "With pleasure. I'll give it to you right away." He stepped into the next room and returned with a small cast-iron donkey. "Here, take it," he said, "Now you have a portrait of me." The canon stared at him in amazement until Escriva explained, "Yes. yes, my friend, that's what I am——a little donkey of the Lord."[2]

I was amused to discover that university teachers, like myself, also bear a family resemblance to the beast of burden, for, on another occasion, Blessed Josemaria wrote:

> For me all donkeys have the bearing of a professor.
> With those splendid ears, that seem like television antennae,
> And that bright and alert look.
> But besides, it's clear that they are wise because they are docile,
> They let themselves be led.[3]

This passage convinced me that the university is for donkeys, not those "old, stubborn, vicious one[s] that would give you a kick when you least expected," but those young ones that are "hard-working and [have] a quick, cheerful trot."[4] Blessed Josemaria's comments were inspired by the verses of Psalm 73: "I was like a donkey in your presence. But I am always with you. You hold my right hand. You guide me with your counsel and afterward you will receive me to glory." It was a donkey, moreover, that Christ chose as a throne when he presented himself to the people as king.

I will translate Blessed Josemaria's ideas freely by using his own words, including those spoken when he was Chancellor of the University of Navarre, and try to show how they apply to the daily life of a professor. Like his friend the donkey, the professor should always be on the lookout for that *divine something* hidden in his everyday tasks.[5] In practical terms this means "there is no

---

[1] *Conversations with Monsignor Escriva de Balaguer*, par.77.

[2] Peter Berglar, *Opus Dei: Life and Works of its Founder, Josemaria Escriva*, pp. 253-254.

[3] *Ut Iumentum*. General Archives of the Prelature (AGP), P01, 1975, p. 1590.

[4] *Christ is Passing By*, 181.

[5] cf. *Conversations*, 121.

excuse for those who could be scholars and are not."[6] If I am to serve God with my mind, then I must realize that "an hour of study, for a modern apostle, is an hour of prayer."[7] This intellectual work, if it is to please God like the fragrant sacrifice of Abel, will "have been shaped through deep study and surrender to [divine] Wisdom."[8] I should be "eager to make [my] pupils understand quickly what has cost [me] hours of study to see clearly."[9] By increasing their understanding, they will conclude that there can be no conflict between faith and science, faith and culture, since "the light of reason comes from God and cannot contradict the light of revelation."[10] The mind will then ascend from natural truths to contemplating their Creator. In order to facilitate this process, I must imitate my brother donkey and put up my ears, like *supernatural antennae*,[11] ready to hear my Master's voice and "to receive the truth of Christ as a light that orientates both action and conduct."[12] As a "privileged cultivator of Knowledge, in love with Truth,"[13] I have a duty to counteract ignorance, which is the worst enemy of God.[14] I teach people, not books, and I must bear witness to those I come into contact with. I am called to be a fisher of men since "men——like fish——have to be caught by the head."[15] People who do mostly headwork, intellectuals, are, as Blessed Josemaria used to say, like "snow-covered mountain peaks: when the snow melts, down comes the water that makes the valleys fruitful."[16] Scholars, in other words, cannot lock themselves up in an ivory tower; their sanctified labour has to act as leaven for the good of society as a whole. In this way Christ will reign at the *summit* of their intellectual activities.[17]

This is indeed a noble human ideal, but one, I admit, that several times I fall short of attaining. I tend to complain that there are too many lectures to prepare, too many tests and papers to mark, too many committee meetings to attend, too many books to read and articles to write, too many colleagues and

---

[6]*The Way*, 332.

[7]*The Way*, 336, 335.

[8]*Forge*, 43.

[9]*Furrow*, 229.

[10]Letter of January 9, 1951, No. 6.

[11]cf. *Forge*, 510.

[12] Address at the investiture of doctors *honoris causa* by the University of Navarre, May 9, 1974. In *Josemaria Excrivá de Balaguer y la Universidad*. EUNSA, 1993, p. 87. St. Josemaria himself received an honorary doctorate from the University of Saragosa in 1960. He placed the ring he was given to mark the occasion on the ear of a small terracotta figure of a donkey that decorated the room where he worked in Rome.

[13]Address at the investiture doctors *honoris causa* by the University of Navarre, October 7, 1967. In *op. cit.*, 87.

[14]cf. *Forge*, no. 635.

[15]*The Way*, 978.

[16]Andres Vazquez de Prada, *The Founder of Opus Dei: The Life of Josemaria Escriva. Volume I: The Early Years*, Princeton, N.J., 2001, p. 199.

[17]cf. *Forge*, 678, 685.

students to see. I become lazy and fulfill to the letter St. Jerome's dictum: "Experience shows that when a donkey is tired it sits down at every corner."[18] These lamentations are the strident brays of an angry and restless donkey that could be translated as "I've had enough!"[19]

At other times, I think I am no longer an *ordinary donkey* with only *average intelligence.*[20] I want to shine before men and steal their applause for myself. I no longer let Jesus use my mind as His throne. So I dream "vain and childish dreams, like those of Tartarin of Tarascon—-imagining [I am] hunting lions" in university corridors, "where the most [I] will find are mice, if that."[21] I become a legend in my own mind, and forget that professors can publish and publish and still perish. I become self-satisfied and unpleasant, making my "knowledge incompatible with good manners." I remain a scholar, but one fit to "be tied to a stall, like a mule."[22] In this sorry state I do not allow my Master to carry out his plan to make me a saint.

But when the Master sees me "so out of sorts, he gives a hearty, understanding laugh." I then realize how silly and futile my antics have been, and how "patient and compassionate towards the failings of men and the rough manners of donkeys"[23] the Master is. I realize, too, that the Master has been playing with me, that all along I have been acting out "a human comedy before a divine spectator."[24] I can't help but think of my beloved Dante and his *Divine Comedy.* My heart is filled with joy because I know the donkey's story has a happy ending: he dies working for his Master. I remember that I have a part in this Ageless Story, that I am called to make "heroic verse out of the prose of each day."[25] Yes, donkeys are very much like Tolkien's hobbits, I tell myself: when they are weak, then they are strong.[26] With this consoling thought I go back to the drawing board. Through love, "a power far greater than that of the legendary King Midas, who changed all he touched into gold," I can change my ordinary activities into "something that will last forever."[27] My time on earth is indeed "a treasure of glory."[28] And I realize that I love to learn so that I can learn to love, *more and better.*

---

18 Quoted in Francis Fernandez, *In Conversation with God*, Volume Three, Princeton, N.J., 1990, p. 217.

19 *Ut lumentum*, AGP, P01, 1975, p. 1585.

20 *Ut lumentum*, AGP, P01, 1975, p. 1586.

21 Friends of God, 8.

22 *The Way*, 350.

23 *Ut lumentum*, AGP, P01, 1975, p. 1585.

24 Friends of God, 152.

25 *Conversations*, 116.

26 cf. I Cor. 1: 27.

27 *Forge*, 742.

28 *Friends of God*, 54

MAY HARTLEY

WORK AND FAMILY—AND SANCTITY TOO

I hope no one thinks that the title of this talk is an advertisement of how I have successfully combined work, family and sanctity too. Perhaps exclamation

St. Josemaria at Villa Sachetti, Rome, April 6, 1971

marks should have been used, or the upper case symbols on the keyboard that are the sign for frustration in the cartoon strips. The title of this talk was actually chosen to reflect the impatience and the normal frustration that arises when we initially think about making God a bigger part of our already busy life. There are days when we all have so much to do and are so busy at work that it takes all our effort to maintain our sanity. To this we add the need to be calm and serene in our family life—as if we can even think about being calm and serene. We are then expected to top it all off with some sanctity, like icing on a cake!! The first temptation may be to say, "Get real."

Then I realised that one of the big things that Opus Dei has done for me is to change my modus operandi. The starting point is neither my work nor my family. The starting point is sanctity, the opposite end of my original focus. The day is viewed from the point of what God is asking of me on this day, from this work, at this particular time.

When I was asked to give this talk, it seemed simple enough. Just talk about Opus Dei and what it has meant in your life. As I have been a member of Opus Dei for quite a few years it didn't seem too difficult. Just relate a few anecdotes. Talk a bit about how it impacted on my family and that should fill the time with ten to fifteen minutes left for questions and discussions. Then I began to think about which anecdotes I would tell. It seemed that they were all too personal for such a public forum. These stories would be about my most intimate joys and sorrows. No way could I talk about them in public. I get very uncomfortable at the thought of speaking about my personal life. I also cry when I recall some particularly rough places when I felt the warm affection of the members of the work looking after me and mine—all the members, including the now deceased prelate, Bishop Alvaro del Portillo, and the current prelate, Bishop Javier Echevarria. So the safest route seemed to be to talk objectively about what I have learned and what I am struggling to practice.

When I met the Work in my early thirties, I was your average, overwhelmed wife and mother who did not understand any of this. I was a typical product of the '70's. The really burning issues were how to save the world from the evils of pollution and over-population. This from someone who had not learned how to get matched pairs of socks from the dryer into the bedrooms. Dinner at a regular hour was not even on the radar. The children's lunches were put together as they were heading out the door to catch the school bus. Somehow I was not living in the real world

What I have since learned is that life is a complicated bit of business. The call to sanctity is not just a call to say more prayers in the day. We are called to sanctify the total package—the spiritual, physical, emotional and intellectual aspects of my life, because they are intertwined. A lack of sleep makes the whole world unbearable. One difficult child can upset the balance of the entire family. Even tracing the effects of trying to practice a particular virtue is difficult because the other virtues increase simultaneously. It is so easy to become confused and not know where to start.

For me the first steps were confession and spiritual direction to get things into perspective. Like most people I suppose, I expected a spiritual director to peer into my soul and tell me what to do with my life, how to pray and be happy all the time, or how to get to heaven with a minimum of effort. Nothing remotely like that ever happened. Instead, I had to make an effort. Imagine! I had to work at this. Nobody ever told me what to do about *anything* unless I asked. Even then, I only received suggestions about personal sanctity and apostolate.

I had to make an effort to make myself understood. Both as I was, sometimes really vile, and as I wanted to be, totally unrealistic, up there with the angels. It was all about openness—mine; making a few decisions—mine; and choosing one or two to put into practice for a couple of weeks—again my responsibility. I guess you could say it was all about me! Of course these all dealt with spiritual situations and apostolate but there was a spill over effect.

The founder of Opus Dei, St. Josemaria Escriva, realised that if people were to do things well they needed to learn *how* to do them. As a result of his foresight, courses on Catholic doctrine, the role and dignity of women in modern society, professional work, including such things as household management (thanks heavens) and time management, were offered at the women's centre. This was not just the effective use of an agenda. From these courses I was finally learning to get my life together *and* schedule the agenda accordingly. Meanwhile, a very real problem was how to recreate in my own home the warm, serene atmosphere I found in the Centres. Finally, there was a coming together of what I was living and what I was thinking. I was developing unity of life. Now it was God first, so that I could then care for my husband, family *and* friends, *and* professional work, with an emphasis on professional, meaning well done.

This "work" does not always have to be unpleasant. It can be loving attention to my spouse, appraising one-of-a-kind, million dollar properties, or lobbying on behalf of the so-called traditional family with senior diplomats and committee representatives at the United Nations. All of this is my "work" and normal material for my sanctification.

In the newly discovered reality of my world, putting God first means that wherever I am, I start my day with prayer and Mass. During that time of prayer I consider what kind of a day lies ahead and I schedule some other time for a little more prayer and a few other spiritual practices. This is the backbone of my day whether we are on office time, home time, holiday time, or on committee time at the UN. Now I am bullish on prayer. I now know, from personal experience, when supernatural outlook drops below the horizon I am left on my own. The impatience mounts, the frustrations build, and the quality of life suffers. I suffer and so do those around me. Those upper case symbols appear again! You must have heard people say, "I don't know how you find the time" to do this, that or the other thing. Well, when they say that to me I answer that I pray a lot.

Part of my prayer life is of course devoted to my marriage and family. They are the primary means of my sanctification. Originally my prayers were probably more like, "God give me strength to put up with him—my husband, or them—my children." I had no idea of what real family life was all about. It was only through courses offered by some people that I met at the Opus Dei Centre and the University of Navarre that I discovered the importance and permanent value of normal family life and the marriage relationship. Now my prayer is more like, "Thank you God for this wonderful husband and family. Please help me not to mess up!"

It was with great wonder that I realized that normal family life, well lived, is the ideal environment for the development of children. I discovered the best place for children to grow and develop is within the family. No special equipment is required. A lack of money or the realisation that money does not grow on trees is actually a definite asset. I was reassured to learn that parents are the primary educators of their children and no one can usurp that right. We actually know what is best for our child. Schools and government are supposed to reflect our will and protect our family and not vice versa.

I learned that caring for my husband, in accordance with my vocation to marriage, was less about food and interior decorating than it was about creating a warm home atmosphere and being emotionally present for him. That the greatest gifts that we can give our children are the happy marriage of their parents and some more brothers and sisters. That children grow happier and healthier when the parents put *each other* first, not the children. Raising children is just that. Bringing those tiny, crying, babies to greater heights over a period of time by teaching them values and letting them see *me* struggle to be a better person. Struggling with one's character in order to improve is a life-long reality. The sooner children learn this, the happier they will be. Eventually they will also be nicer people too.

As a woman, I tend to get obsessive about my children or my sick relatives, assuming that my husband will be able to take care of himself. My husband assumes that I will understand his career plan. No one is looking after the shop, as the expression goes. This is a huge mistake both for the husband and the wife. The marriage relationship is the most important relationship for any married person. It is God's plan for married couples. If we look after this, our married life is much happier.

All of the above can be learned by anyone. The previously mentioned Family Enrichment courses have helped many couples all over the world. This includes those who have experienced true family life in a traditional family or those who have not. The latter may have suffered the instability of a common-law union or the divorce of their own parents. It takes a bit of effort but we must also teach these people about their intrinsic worth. About the fact that Christ came and died for them too. Again we are encountering the complexity of the human person.

It was the faith that attracted me to the Work but it was the warmth of the family Opus Dei that initially kept me there. The genuine affection that members have for one another really impressed me. After being at the canonization of Saint Josemaria Escriva I know this family life spans continents, language and politics. After meeting Opus Dei, my social life took a turn for the better. I began to enjoy the good life. Not wine, shopping and holidays, although these are to be enjoyed in moderation. It was the truly good things that I was finally noticing – good people with human virtues, good work well done, good friends, etc.

The book *God and Children* by Jose Urteaga gave me my first inkling that there was something more to raising children than good marks in school. It was followed by courses on family, conferences on various aspects of family life, and eventually apostolic exhortations and encyclicals. Some of this was because of my interest in family and some was spiritual reading suggested by my spiritual director.

Spiritual reading is a wonderful way of staying connected to a normal world, to the world as it should be. The few minutes of daily spiritual reading has given me some unexpected insights, the first being that saints, just like St. Josemaria Escriva, are wonderful people with a great sense of humour, personal charm and a true understanding of human nature. My spiritual reading includes modern writings as well timeless books such as those by Saint Francis de Sales. In his book, *The Introduction to the Devout Life*, he gives advice to married couples to be devoted to one another. It is interesting that he calls both spouses to be responsible for the other. This is the ideal that the church has always encouraged even before women's rights were an issue.

Something else that I learned is that the parents need to present a united front at home, to the extent that it is better for both parents to be united *and wrong* than for one parent to contradict another in front of the children. This provided me with some very interesting food for thought

All of the above made a huge difference in my daily life. They are things I learned through being in touch with Opus Dei. However, I was also learning more about my faith on the doctrinal level. Truths of my faith became clearer because of the doctrine courses offered at the Centres. Figures in the New Testament suddenly began to take shape and their importance was becoming clearer.

I can remember when the topic of devotion to Our Lady was first raised by my spiritual director. My response was something like, "Yes, Our Lady is nice, but when I pray I prefer to go to God himself. It's more direct." Fortunately, my spiritual director did not give up on me. Over the next several years I learned about the importance of Our Lady in God's plan, how much she truly cares for us, and how much more effective her prayers are than mine alone.

Another figure that has taken shape since being in touch with the Work is St. Joseph. St. Josemaria referred to him as, "Our father and lord". I wondered why. Why was the founder happy when St. Joseph was made the universal patron of the Catholic Church? Now St. Joseph seems to me to be so human, just like any spouse. He was born flawed, not perfect, he does not immediately have all the answers, but he does know when he needs to really think about things. He may not be as gifted as his spouse, but he gave the very best of himself to his wife and family.

These things are useful for any husband and wife to know—with the exception of the wife being more gifted than her husband, of course. There is still a lot to be learned about St. Joseph, but now at least I am beginning to understand why he is important as a role model in the universal church and for the members of Opus Dei.

Another important lesson that I learned is that sanctity also means being united to the Church and its magisterium. The representative of Christ on earth, the Pope, John Paul II, has made this obedience to the church a delightful duty. His travels have made the papacy come alive. He is the Pope who has written most about family. They are no longer just disembodied writings from Rome but the concerns of a loving and loveable, truly holy father. I have found his writings on the role of women in the church and the dignity of women to be enriching and demanding. For anyone who takes the time to read them, one must conclude that these are the answers to protect the rights of women. As a woman I feel uplifted and grateful for this.

When I became a member of Opus Dei, I agreed to fulfil my Christian obligation to help others get closer to God. This was not to be done by mass mailings or media promotion. It was to be done naturally, one on one, with my personal friends. I had an obligation to love and help them in a supernatural way as much as I could. They would then be closer to God and happier as a result. This is a teaching of the Catholic Church. The obligation came with Baptism. Therefore it is not an Opus Dei invention. All that Opus Dei does is help me to fulfil that obligation. But when I first heard this in Opus Dei, I thought it was a cover to increase membership. The fact that God is happiness and getting closer to Him naturally makes one happier, and the fact that the Church has always encouraged the faithful to do apostolate didn't seem to carry much weight with me. Again I was not living in the real world.

Twenty-five years later I realize that what you see and hear in Opus Dei is what you get. There are no ulterior motives or hidden agendas. The only point of Opus Dei is to make people happier by bringing them closer to God. This is done through the normal course of events in our life. We meet people, naturally become friends, and want to make them happier. We spend time with them because of shared interests. In fact the Founder has warned us not to instrumentalise friendship.

For members of Opus Dei, God is a really big part of their life. It is natural that it should be shared as a part of any good friendship. Otherwise, it looks like we are hiding something. When we look at friendship this way, it takes on a whole new dimension and we begin to live in a more integrated way. We begin to live and practice what we think. We begin to have unity of life, live in the real world, and invite our friends to come along.

Apostolate is usually done in this natural way. Other times, for reasons that God alone knows, a chance acquaintance will spark an opportunity to speak of God on the first encounter. This usually happens on a plane or train or some other situation when there is little chance of meeting again. A person will bare their soul because time is limited and by doing so they ask for help. This happened to me recently. In the course of my professional work, I met a single mother. After my work was finished and I was preparing to leave, this lady suddenly blurted out that her life was difficult and she was suffering a lot. At this she fought to hold back tears. Not knowing what to do, I said that I would pray for her. She told me that she didn't believe in prayer and asked if I really did. I said yes and that I would pray for her just the same if it was all right with her. She said, " Yes, thank you .You are very kind." It was a combination of work and sanctity that I had not expected. These situations are unusual, but if God allows them to happen, then he expects us to ask for his grace to resolve them.

There are no cookbook solutions in Opus Dei. Everyone is unique and ultimately one responds to one's own situation in his or her own way. My hope of being told what to do with my life to fast track to heaven did not work because personal freedom and responsibility are virtues that the Founder was adamant about protecting. In his homily, "Christ the King", St. Josemaria says, " There is one value which a ... Christian must particularly cherish; personal freedom. Only if he defends the individual freedom of others—with the personal responsibility that must go with it—only then can he defend his own with human and Christian integrity." There are hundreds of by-laws for the city of

Montreal. There are 111 articles in the Charter of the United Nations. Just think of a life that has only ten rules and six precepts. It is wonderfully free. It is true liberation. We have this wonderful freedom when we follow the laws of God and the precepts of the Church. Everything else is up for discussion. What colour to paint the dining room. When and where to go on vacation. In the eternal scheme of things they don't amount to much. They are not worth fighting about. For any legitimate undertaking, the only thing that matters is how much loving work we put into these decisions. It is the effort not the results that count. Fortunately, God does not ask the impossible and He wants us to be happy.

Opus Dei has taught me how to turn the events of my busy, mostly uneventful life into something of eternal worth: the ordinary things that anyone can do. It taught me to live in the present, fulfilling the will of God in the small things. When this is done, then what we perceive as the big things take care of themselves.

The Founder's greatest devotion was to the Holy Mass and the Blessed Sacrament. His homily "The Eucharist, Mystery of Faith and Love" provides me with many points for meditation. His writings encourage me to attend Mass, to learn to love the Mass, and to increase my devotion to the Holy Eucharist as a lifelong goal. He also taught me about unity of life, and about trying to think of God's will before, during, and after my actions. All of these teachings are the basis of a continuing struggle and a strength for me. All of them are one hundred percent in keeping with the teachings of the Catholic Church.

It does not seem to matter how many times I read the writings of St. Josemaria, there are always new insights. I would like to end by listing some of the conclusions about my own life and about Opus Dei that I have been led to by those writings. You may have come to some of these conclusions yourselves.

First, the more I think about others, the happier I am. It is a standard joke amongst some of my busy friends that someday, we will have a day off to have our turning-thirty crisis, our turning-forty angst, our mid-life crisis, and our children-leaving-home breakdown. We cannot allocate more than one day because we are too busy. To date, none of us have found the time or the inclination.

Second, marriage is a marvellous gift from God. He has seen fit to allow me to freely choose the person that I want to love for the rest of my life and He has crowned my decision with the promise of the jewel of eternity.

Third, raising a child is the most satisfying and challenging task in the world. There are no guarantees. A parent is a parent 24-7.

Fourth, Opus Dei is a radical organisation in as much as it demands a fundamental change in one's understanding of the importance of God, and then the effort to live that belief. Most people do not use the word radical in this sense.

Fifth, people in the Work really do come from all walks of life. There are many families who manage to be elegant and well mannered. This has less to do with wealth then it does with good taste and managing the home well.

Sixth, the Work encourages women and men to live a responsible, balanced life with God, spouse, and children as the first priorities. This includes any working arrangement that benefits the spouse and family. With a popular cartoon strip devoted to the life of a stay at home husband, this arrangement is no longer a rarity. Wherever they work, men and women need to try to sanctify what they are doing.

Seventh, in the Work, one is very free to choose profession and state in life. There are women such as myself in traditionally male occupations as well as women who want to be wives and mothers. But in Opus Dei there is only one vocation – a universal call to sanctity. For those who wish to remain single, Opus Dei offers a tantalising possibility: An unmarried person can be completely dedicated to God while doing their professional work and maintaining their lay status. Without a spouse and children, they live a warm family life in the Centres of the Work.

Eighth, and finally, all vocations are demanding. There are no easy ways to get to heaven. Whether we live married life, or the celibate life, God always asks something of us. He also rewards us far beyond our small sacrifices. That is just here on this earth. What awaits us in heaven is rather delicious to think about but impossible to imagine.

In summary, becoming a member of Opus Dei has changed my world dramatically. What I was looking for, without realising it, was a greater meaning to my life. I have certainly found it. It has introduced me to the writings of the popes and saints of the church and given me a better understanding of my faith. It has enriched my marriage, helped to convert my husband to Catholicism, helped in the character development of my children through the various clubs and camps, and made me understand the beauty of my vocation to marriage. It has also made me appreciate the permanent value of family. As a result of the teachings of St. Josemaria, I try to be a more loyal friend and more grateful for the friendship that others extend to me. I have better respect for the freedom of others and view differences as just that, differences, and not barriers or arguments to be won.

This did not happen overnight. I am not a saint. My husband, children and family are here and they will attest to that. There are no saints on earth. However I am one hundred percent sure that if I persevere in Opus Dei, I will eventually get to heaven. In the meantime, life is happier and more meaningful than it was. Every aspect of life presents challenges. I don't know what lies ahead but I do know that whatever happens, there will always be joy. I feel privileged to be here to tell you about some of these things. Everyone's life is different but the grace and joy of God awaits us all.

THE HOMILY GIVEN BY POPE JOHN PAUL II AT THE MASS OF
CANONIZATION FOR ST. JOSEMARIA ESCRIVA, OCTOBER 6, 2002,
WITH A REPORT OF THE CEREMONY FROM
L'OSSERVATORE ROMANO

On Sunday, 6 October, in St Peter's Square, before one of the largest and most
orderly groups of pilgrims, the Holy Father canonized St Josemaria Escriva de
Balaguer, founder of Opus Dei, and called his message of sanctifying daily life
valid for all believers. Police said that at least 300,000 people were packed into
St Peter's Square and nearby streets, where huge speakers and video screens
allowed them to follow the Mass. The crowd was silent while the Pope read the
Latin formula of canonization, but as soon as he finished the trumpets sounded, the choir sang a series of Alleluias and the crowd erupted in cheers that
bounced off the buildings around the square. After the proclamation, the Pope
received a relic of St Josemaria that was placed on a stand near the lectern for
the singing of the Gospel. A huge portrait decorated with flowers adorned the
facade of St Peter's and there were magnificent floral tapestries covering the
steps in front of the main altar. The canonization came 27 years after St
Josemaria's death in 1975. Beatified in 1992, the saint was approved for canonization after the Holy Father accepted a miracle attributed to his intercession.
It involved the medically unexplainable 1992 cure of a Spanish physician,
Manuel Nevado Rey, suffering from a progressive skin disease resulting from
years of exposure to radiation from X-ray machines. High level government
delegations from Spain, Italy, Kenya and more than a dozen South American
countries were present at the Mass, as well as non-Catholic delegations and
representatives of other ecclesial movements. Organizers said the canonization
was attended by people from at least 84 countries. Pilgrims from Spain and
Italy formed the largest groups followed by those from Mexico, South
America, Germany, United States and France. Many Italian commentators
remarked on the orderliness and prayerfulness of the pilgrims. Many pilgrims
knelt on the cobblestones during the consecration. Young persons carrying
white umbrellas accompanied the priests to their communion stations and kept
the umbrellas over the priests while they distributed communion to the pilgrims. At the end of the Mass, before the Angelus, the Holy Father greeted the
pilgrims in their own languages. After the blessing, to greet the pilgrims, the
Holy Father traveled the length of the Via della Conciliazione in an open car.

THE HOMILY

1. "All who are led by the Spirit of God are sons of God" (Rom 8,14). These
   words of the Apostle Paul, which we have just heard, help us understand

better the significant message of today's canonization of Josemaria Escriva de Balaguer. With docility he allowed himself to be led by the Spirit, convinced that only in this way can one fully accomplish God's will.

This fundamental Christian truth was a constant theme in his preaching. Indeed, he never stopped inviting his spiritual children to invoke the Holy Spirit to ensure that their interior life, namely, their life of relationship with God and their family, professional and social life, totally made up of small earthly realities, would not be separated but would form only one life that was "holy and full of God." He wrote, "We find the invisible God in the most visible and material things" (Conversations with Josemaria Escriva, n. 114).

This teaching of his is still timely and urgent today. In virtue of the Baptism that incorporates him into Christ, the believer is called to establish with the Lord an uninterrupted and vital relationship. He is called to be holy and to collaborate in the salvation of humanity.

2. "The Lord God took the man and put him in the garden of Eden to till it and keep it" (Gn 2,15). The Book of Genesis, as we heard in the first reading, reminds us that the Creator has entrusted the earth to man, to "till" it and "keep" it. Believers acting in the various realities of this world contribute to realize this divine universal plan. Work and any other activity, carried out with the help of grace, is converted into a means of daily sanctification.

"The ordinary life of a Christian who has faith", Josemaría Escrivá used to say, "when he works or rests, when he prays or sleeps, at all times, is a life in which God is always present" (Meditations, 3 March 1954). This supernatural vision of life unfolds an extraordinarily rich horizon of salvific perspectives, because, even in the only apparently monotonous flow of normal earthly events, God comes close to us and we can cooperate with his plan of salvation. So it is easier to understand what the Second Vatican Council affirmed: "there is no question, then, of the Christian message inhibiting men from building up the world ... on the contrary it is an incentive to do these very things" (Gaudium et Spes, n. 34).

3. To elevate the world to God and transform it from within: this is the ideal the holy founder points out to you, dear brothers and sisters, who rejoice today to see him raised to the glory of the altars. He continues to remind you of the need not to let yourselves be frightened by a materialist culture that threatens to dissolve the genuine identity of Christ's disciples. He liked to repeat forcefully that the Christian faith is opposed to conformism and interior inertia.

Following in his footsteps, spread in society the consciousness that we are all called to holiness whatever our race, class, society or age. In the first place, struggle to be saints yourselves, cultivating an evangelical style of humility and service, abandonment to Providence and of constant listening to the voice of the Spirit. In this way, you will be the "salt of the earth" (cf. Mt 5,13) and "your light so shine before men, that they may see your good works and give glory to your Father who is in heaven" (ibid., 5,16).

4. Those who want to serve the cause of the Gospel faithfully will certainly encounter misunderstandings and difficulties. The Lord purifies and shapes all those he calls to follow him with the mysterious power of the Cross; but "in the Cross," the new saint repeated, "we find light, peace and joy: *Lux in Cruce, requies in Cruce, gaudium in Cruce!*"

Ever since 7 August 1931 when, during the celebration of holy Mass, the words of Jesus echoed in his soul, "when I am lifted up from the earth, I will draw all to myself" (Jn 12,32), Josemaria Escriva understood more clearly that the mission of the baptized consists in raising the Cross of Christ above all human reality and he felt burning within him the impassioned vocation to evangelize every human setting. Then, without hesitation, he accepted Jesus' invitation to the Apostle Peter, which we just heard in this square: "Duc in altum!" (Put out into the deep). He transmitted it to his entire spiritual family so that they might offer the Church a valid contribution of communion and apostolic service. Today this invitation is extended to all of us: "Put out into the deep," the divine Teacher says to us, "and let down your nets for a catch" (Lk 5,4).

5. To fulfill such a rigorous mission, one needs constant interior growth nourished by prayer. St Josemaría was a master in the practice of prayer, which he considered to be an extraordinary "weapon" to redeem the world. He always recommended: "In the first place prayer; then expiation; in the third place, but very much in third place, action" (The Way, n. 82). It is not a paradox but a perennial truth: the fruitfulness of the apostolate lies above all in prayer and in intense and constant sacramental life. This, in essence, is the secret of the holiness and the true success of the saints.

May the Lord help you, dear brothers and sisters, to accept this challenging ascetical and missionary instruction. May Mary sustain you, whom the holy founder invoked as "*Spes nostra, Sedes Sapientiae, Ancilla Domini!*" (Our Hope, Seat of Wisdom, Handmaid of the Lord).

May Our Lady make everyone an authentic witness of the Gospel, ready everywhere to make a generous contribution to building the Kingdom of Christ! May the example and teaching of St Josemaría be an incentive to us so that at the end of the earthly pilgrimage, we too may be able to share in the blessed inheritance of heaven! There, together with the angels and all the saints, we will contemplate the face of God and sing his glory for all eternity.

WRITINGS OF ST. JOSEMARIA ESCRIVA FREQUENTLY CITED IN THIS VOLUME

The Way, Princeton: Scepter, 2001, first published by Scepter in 1957.

Furrow, London-New York: Scepter, 1987.

The Forge, London-New York: Scepter, 1987.

Friends of God, London-New York: Scepter, 1981.

Christ is Passing By, New York: Scepter, 1984.

Conversations with Msg. Josemaria Escriva de Balaguer, Sydney: Little Hills & Scepter, 1993.

These writings can be found on the internet at www.escrivaworks.org.

For further information about St. Josemaria, consult:

Peter Berglar, *Opus Dei, Life and Work of its Founder,* Princeton: Scepter, 1994.

C. Cavalleri, *Immersed in God, Blessed Josemaría Escrivá, as seen by his successor, Bishop Alvaro del Portillo,* Princeton: Scepter, 1996.

John F. Coverdale, *Uncommon Faith: The Early Years of Opus Dei (1928-1943),* Princeton: Scepter, 2002.

Andrés Vásquez de Prada, *The Founder of Opus Dei, The Life of Josemaría Escrivá,* 2 vols., Princeton: Scepter, Inc., 2001 and 2002.

About our Authors

John Haas,, Ph.D., S.T.L., is President of the National Catholic Bioethics Center of the United States. He has been Professor of Moral Theology in several seminaries, and has lectured extensively in the United States and other countries, including Peru, Mexico, Germany, Switzerland, Italy, Canada, and the Vatican.

Rev. Joseph Soria, M.D., J.C.D., was St. Josemaria's personal physician for many years. Formerly Professor of Pastoral Medicine and *Catholicae Doctrinae Expositio* in the Pontifical Lateran University, he is author of more than 15 books and booklets, and more that 60 articles.

John F. Coverdale, Ph.D., J.D., is Professor of Law at Seton Hall University. He has taught history at Princeton and Northwestern Universities, and written several books on Spanish history, most recently *Uncommon Faith, The Early Years on Opus Dei (1928-1943)*, Scepter, 2002.

Carlos Cavallé, Ph.D., is Anselmo Rubiralta Professor of Business Administration at the IESE Business School, Barcelona. He is also Chairman of Euroforum El Esconal and president of several research centres. IESE's programmes are consistently ranked among the very best in the world.

Jenny Driver, M.D., is certified in Internal Medicine and is continuing her training in Hematology and Oncology at the Beth Israel Deaconess Medical Center in Boston. She is Instructor in Medicine at Harvard Medical School, where she is involved in teaching and research.

Clifford Orwin, Ph.D., is Professor of Political Science at the University of Toronto. His many publications include important books on Thucydides and Rousseau. He is a regular columnist for the *National Post.*

Cecelia Royals is the President of The National Institute of Womanhood in Washington, D.C. She has testified before U. S. Senate and Congressional Committees and has addressed groups in many countries, including Argentina, Uganda, France, Spain, China, and Honduras, on issues pertaining to the status of women.

Rev. Msgr. John Murphy, P.H., J.C.D., is Chancellor of Spiritual Affairs, Archdiocese of Toronto. After receiving a Master of Divinity degree from the University of Toronto, he completed a Licentiate and a Doctorate in Canon law at the Pontifical Lateran University.

Graeme Hunter, Ph.D., is Professor of Philosophy at the University of Ottawa, and Professor of Philosophy and Literature at Augustine College,

Ottawa. In 1998-99, he held the Father Edo Gatto Chair of Christian Studies at St. Francis Xavier University, Antigonish, Nova Scotia.

M. Sharon Hefferan, M.B.A., is Director of the Metro Achievement Center, an educational enrichment program for economically disadvantaged inner city girls in Chicago. Ms. Hefferan has dedicated her efforts to social programmes in New York, Milwaukee, Lithuania, and Chicago.

Anthony Yeow was a founding member and is a board member of Toronto Youth Development, which provides academic and sports enrichment programmes for boys and for girls in Regent Park, the largest public housing development in Canada.

Mrs. May Hartley is the mother of four children and grandmother of seven. Her first love was, and still is, her family. She has served on the national board of Family Development in Canada since 1985 and as a director for the International Federation for Family Development since its inception in 1998. She has taught real estate appraisal at the college level and chaired committees for the Appraisal Institute. She now spends her free time lobbying for the traditional family at the United Nations.

Dominic Manganiello, D. Phil., is Professor of English Literature at the University of Ottawa. He is the author of *Joyce's Politics* and *T.S. Eliot and Dante*, and co-author of *Rethinking the Future of the University*. He has also published articles on G.K. Chesterton, J.R.R. Tolkien, C.S. Lewis, and Dorothy L. Sayers.

Teresa A. Tomory, Ph.D., is the mother of seven children, and Head of Hawthorn School for Girls, an independent school in Toronto. She is one of the founding members of Hawthorn, and was a member of the organizing committee for the Second Pan American Conference on Family and Education, held in Toronto in 1996. She is a member of the Board of Directors of Patrons of the Arts in the Vatican Museums, Canadian Chapter, and has published articles in archaeology and art history.

AGMV Marquis

MEMBER OF SCABRINI MEDIA

Quebec, Canada